Thoughtful gardening

Thoughtful gardening

Ed Ikin

National Trust

Dedication: *For Bill*

First published in the United Kingdom in 2010 by
National Trust Books
10 Southcombe Street
London
W14 0RA

An imprint of Anova Books Company Ltd

Copyright © National Trust Books, 2010
Text © Ed Ikin, 2010
The moral rights of the author have been asserted.

Illustrations by Alan Hancocks

ISBN: 9781905400942

A CIP catalogue record for this book is available from the
British Library.

20 19 18 17 16 15 14 13 12 11 10
10 9 8 7 6 5 4 3 2 1

Reproduction by Mission, Hong Kong
Printed by 1010 International Printing Ltd, China

This book can be ordered direct from the publisher at
the website www.anovabooks.com, or try your local
bookshop. Also available at National Trust shops and
www.nationaltrustbooks.co.uk.

Mixed Sources
Product group from well-managed
forests, controlled sources and
recycled wood or fibre
www.fsc.org Cert no. SGS-COC-003963
© 1996 Forest Stewardship Council
FSC

Contents

Introduction

Since the beginning of human civilisation, the most successful gardeners have worked in tandem with the natural forces found in every garden and plant. A beautiful flower can charm and thrill – but you should only really be satisfied if it is borne on a strong, healthy plant, growing in the right place.

The more we know about plants, soil and water, the better we can create gardens that thrive with minimal intervention from us. There is nothing wrong with being scientific! It's not embarrassing to know your soil type and condition, how quickly your garden goes from flood to drought, whether it drops to -10°C in the winter or has troublesome hotspots.

Is this a book about green gardening? It is about the most satisfying type of gardening: efficient and beautiful, suited to your conditions and requiring the minimum of intervention. Terms such as 'green' and 'organic' only tell part of the story. This book is not about scruffiness, old carpets, car tyres and nettles or any of the other rather negative images associated with being green. It is about presenting a garden to the highest standard, in harmony with nature.

Butterflies thrive in any diverse garden.

6

There are practical reasons why a thoughtful approach to gardening is required. Climate change gives us periods of drought, torrential deluges of rain and winters that alternate from frost-free to bitterly cold. Our plants need to be in the best shape to adapt to these varying conditions, and we need to find clever approaches to reduce our own environmental footprint. The chemical route for gardeners is narrowing all the time. As legislation tightens, fewer and fewer pesticides are available, forcing all of us to look for effective alternatives.

what is a thoughtful gardener?

The answer to this question is someone who knows how their garden works. The thoughtful gardener understands the basic principles that govern soil, water and plants and turns them into flowers, fruit and healthy gardens. Some of their choices may not be from the mainstream but there will be sound theory behind them.

Throughout this book, I will look at the choices a thoughtful gardener can make, from selecting the right plant for the right place to creating an ecologically balanced lawn. I hope it will provide a deeper understanding of how gardens function, give you the information and inspiration to try a new way of gardening, or simply add new techniques to your already thoughtful approach.

Would you rather have your cake and eat it? Would you like to have a stunning, distinctive garden that rewards your creative instincts but does not cost the earth? If so, read on…

Soil

I would love to start this chapter by regaling you with tales of beautiful exotic plants, but I cannot. To write successfully about gardening, I have to start by looking beyond colour, foliage and form and instead scrutinise the muddy brown stuff plants grow in. The secret is truly in the soil.

what is soil?

Soil is more complex than it first appears. The main constituents are mineral particles, either silt (fine), sand (coarse) or clay (somewhere in-between). Between the mineral particles are spaces known as pores and these are either full of water or air. Good soils contain organic matter: the composted remains of plants or animals. The final element is alive: a host of microscopic organisms.

Soil serves a multitude of purposes and it is helpful for the thoughtful gardener to know what they are.

Soil is essential for plants to anchor their roots.

Anchorage

Superficially soil is an anchor, a foundation for plant roots to grip into as they seek to thrust themselves skywards. The physical variations within soil mean that this role occurs with varying degrees of success, although the sheer diversity of the plant kingdom ensures that even desert sand and coarse Mediterranean gravel can still provide the means for a plant to anchor itself. So is this all we need to know? Is soil just somewhere for a plant to stick its roots?

Microscopic allies

Soil is one of the most profoundly complex biological entities in the natural world. A teaspoon of typical 'wild' soil can contain up to one billion microbes, composed of many hundreds of different species. Many of these microbes, as will be explained below, are inextricably linked to plants and have evolved alongside them, forming relationships of mutual benefit (for more on wild soil, see page 14).

Water

Plants are composed of up to 90 per cent water and virtually all of this is drawn from the soil. Although it may look uniform, soil is very diverse in its structure and this creates a network of air pockets (also known as pores) that fill with water. Plant roots seek out water and draw it up into leaves and shoots using sophisticated engineering.

Nutrients

In order to grow, plants need a wide variety of different nutrients in extremely exacting quantities, and these all have to be drawn from the soil. Just as people and animals quickly become ill when deprived of certain vitamins, plants cannot tolerate nutrient deficiency and display symptoms such as discoloured leaves, distorted growth and failed fruits and flowers (for more information, see page 110).

different soil types

Does it matter what sort of soil you have? Why bother finding out? The reason it is worth becoming a soil geek is simple: know your soil, master your garden. Much time and effort can be exerted and wasted if you are gardening a soil in the wrong way. Are you ever going to successfully grow Mediterranean plants on a boggy clay soil? Or are you still trying to establish bog plants on free-draining, thin sand?

Soils fall into three main types: sand, clay and silt. Silt soils are unusual and most gardeners work with sand, clay or something in-between. The type of soil that we dig and plant into is fundamentally dictated by the rock that lies beneath and the majority of gardens seem to have soil with some undesirable characteristic, challenging the gardener in us to find clever, flexible strategies that allow our plants to thrive.

Soil can be composed of sand, clay or silt, or a combination of these three soil types.

100% clay   0% silt

CLAY

50% clay   sandy clay   silty clay   50% silt

clay loam

sandy loam   silt loam

0% clay   100% silt

SAND   LOAM   SILT

100% sand   50% sand   0% sand

Sandy soils

Sandy soils are composed of large, coarse particles of sand and silica. The easiest way to identify a sandy soil is to rub some between your fingers: does it feel gritty and abrasive? Does the sound of the particles rubbing together remind you of being on a beach? If so, you have a sandy soil.

The benefits

The key characteristic of a sandy soil is its drainage. Just hours after heavy rain, puddles have gone and the soil can be worked and walked upon, allowing access all winter. The large, unevenly shaped particles never sit together tightly or uniformly and this creates a large network of pores. With the sand particles holding no strong attraction to water molecules, rain rushes through the pores and away.

The 'dryness' of this soil type and the physical nature of the sand particles endow sandy soils with another desirable characteristic: the ability to heat up quickly. Without large volumes of water to 'warm', the soil responds readily to the sun, allowing spring gardening to start early.

The drawbacks

Now for the bad news: rapid drainage may allow gardeners with sandy soil to work in all seasons, but this is not always great for our plants. Young trees with weak root systems struggle to draw in water efficiently. With water rushing through the soil at high speed, there is simply not enough time to drink: this can result in sudden wilting. A spring-planted garden on a thin, sandy soil could be lost in a drought situation, surely an incentive to take great care with plant choices and planting times.

Equally undesirable is the tendency of sandy soil to lose nutrients and organic matter. It sometimes feels like a losing battle as barrow-loads of manure seemingly evaporate into hungry, sandy soils and applications of fertiliser last barely a week on lawns.

What always thwarts efforts on sandy soil is a result of the chemistry of opposite attraction. Whereas clay soils are covered in minute electric charges, which can bind on to oppositely charged fertilisers, sandy soils have no such facility, and cannot hold on to nutrients without help. Knowing you have a sandy soil should influence what you add – fertilisers will be wasted unless the soil has been improved with regular additions of organic matter (see page 26).

Soil pH dictates which groups of plants will grow best in your soil and the rather acidic nature of sandy soils (with a pH of anything from three to neutral) means a large range of fruit and vegetables, plus some of the finest flowering plants, can grow without the need for chemical intervention to alter the pH.

Clay soils

Clay soils come with a reputation for being hard work. Heavy in texture, with a tendency to hold lots of water, any gardener who digs clay soil for years builds strong muscles. Clay soils also exhibit an extreme range of behaviour; their 'plastic' inflexible nature makes them heavy and sticky in the winter and ready to crack open in the first dry spell of spring or summer.

The amount of water in clay soils makes them very cold after winter and their slowness to warm up impedes early spring sowings. Clay particles are a lot finer than sand and have the ability to bind together, making a lovely 'crumb' structure in well-worked soils and horrible heavy 'clods' in poorly worked ones.

So is it a disaster if your garden has clay soil?

Far from it. The first step for the thoughtful gardener is to focus on the right groups of plants. Roses will thrive, herbaceous plants fond of a heavier soil (such as *Aruncus*, *Monarda* and *Ligularia*) will be happy, as will many shrubs. As soon as you realise that plants such as lavender, rosemary and aloes will not grow well, then most frustrations with clay will end.

Clay soils respond wonderfully to good gardening. By adding plenty of bulky organic matter such as composted stable manure (see page 27), the heavy plates and clods of clay start to break down into something far more manageable. The key is to dig organic matter into the rooting area (around a spade's depth) prior to planting and not to skimp on quantities. The process of digging in this much organic matter will make the soil level rise dramatically as it becomes more bulky and full of air. This is a desirable trait as it shows the soil is changing in character. If there is too much of it, skim off the top layer and use elsewhere.

In-between

In-between the two extremes of sand and clay lie a multitude of variations. Some are better for gardening on than others. The holy grail of soils is a sandy loam: free-draining but able to hold useful quantities of water, fertile, deep and willing to bind fertilisers and organic matter.

While a sandy loam may be a huge advantage, it should be noted how many great public gardens are on 'poor' soils, from the thin sand at RHS Wisley in Surrey to the chalk at Highdown in West Sussex and the heavy clay of Sissinghurst in Kent.

the perfect soil

The perfect 'wild' soil will support a wide variety of plants without the need for pesticides or fertilisers. Diseases are suppressed, predators out-competed (or eaten), while naturally occurring nutrients are regularly and consistently available. How is this possible when we need to add fertiliser and pesticides to make our own gardens work?

This is all down to a healthy 'soil flora' and a balanced 'soil food web'. The soil flora are a diverse group of micro-organisms that form beneficial relationships with plants, offering services in return for plant 'waste' products such as sugars. A balanced 'soil food web' involves the interaction of fungi, bacteria, nematodes and protozoa. On the following pages is a summary of their role in healthy soil.

Habitats such as woodlands have perfect 'wild' soils.

Fungi

There is much more to fungi than the toadstools and mushrooms that pop up every autumn. A vast network of thin tendrils exist underground, working their way through the soil and feeding on sugars exuded by plant roots and rotting organic matter such as dead wood. Occasionally they reproduce by popping a 'fruiting body' above ground, which we would refer to as a toadstool. The world's largest organism is a honey fungus, a 2,400-year-old example that lives in the Strawberry Mountains of Oregon. This giant is some $8.9km^2$ ($3\frac{1}{2}miles^2$) – considerably bigger than a blue whale.

Fungi occupy much of the ground below and yet are virtually invisible to us. They have evolved alongside plants for thousands of years and formed complex, inter-dependent relationships known as symbioses. Many of these relationships are of great benefit to plants, others of great harm, and while this is a gross simplification, it is useful to split them into two groups: good fungi and bad fungi.

Good fungi

Good fungi form associations with the roots of plants, making roots more efficient in the uptake of nutrients and water. Some fungi will weave

Fruiting bodies, such as this morel mushroom, can be evidence of larger underground organisms.

themselves around the plant, massively increasing the size of the root system, and allowing water and nutrients to be taken up with much greater efficiency.

In some plants, the relationship with fungi has been taken to the point where the plant literally cannot exist without them. Some orchid seed has no 'food' in it at all, and the developing seedling gets all its food from a fungal friend. Without it, it could not grow.

Humans can benefit greatly from the long-standing plant-fungi alliance. White oaks in France and Italy are often planted in rows, with the owners knowing this particular tree associates with the truffle fungus. As the fungus develops, it eventually starts to produce fruiting bodies, which are promptly harvested and sold to restaurants around the world.

Good fungi also mop up waste sugars exuded by plant roots to ensure nothing is left for disease fungi to feed on; in fact their mere presence in the 'rootzone' of plants means there is far less space for undesirable organisms to occupy.

Bad fungi

Honey fungus, blight, black spot: this is an ugly roll-call of undesirable threats to our beloved garden plants. How can fungi – that in some cases are essential to plant life – be killers too?

For some fungi, the temptation to explore a plant's vulnerabilities is too strong. If there is room around the roots to occupy, honey fungus will not need a second invitation. The strong dynamic tendrils that are used to travelling through miles of soil are equally adept at entering a plant and colonising trunks, branches and twigs.

17

Honey fungus can be an aggressive organisism that attacks tree roots and colonises trunks.

An ancient oak tree will literally be full of fungi, some good, some bad, and it will live for centuries with these tenants. Then something snaps. A change occurs in either tree or fungus and the harmonious balance is gone. When behaving aggressively, honey fungus will quickly consume living plant tissue and shut down roots.

Bacteria

We tend to think of bacteria in negative terms, but they play a vital role in healthy soil. Their ability to break down certain forms of organic material, such as cellulose, from plants is unrivalled and the end product is useful for plants. One group of bacteria, the actinomycetes, bond soil particles together using fine filaments, allowing 'tired' soil structures to be rebuilt.

The *Rhizobia* bacteria are well known to growers of peas and beans. These microscopic individuals live on the root nodules of legumes and 'fix' nitrogen into a form useful to all plants.

Another group of bacteria, the genus *Bacillus*, has been harnessed by us to 'vaccinate' plants against disease, but more of that later (see pages 73–74).

Protozoa

Protozoa are voracious eaters and move freely in the soil, 'swimming' using fine, oscillating hairs. In healthy soil, protozoa 'graze' on bacteria to maintain them at desirable levels. As they eat, they release waste nitrogen, which is freely available for plants to use.

Nematode worms

Nematodes exist in vast numbers throughout the soil. A hugely varied group, nematodes such as eelworms cause devastation to potato and daffodil crops, while others are invaluable garden allies, controlling slugs, vine weevils and caterpillars.

We need plenty of good nematodes and fewer of the bad. Some nematodes are aggressive predators with strong jaws and will happily prey upon 'bad' nematodes such as eelworm. Another group of nematodes play a similar role to protozoa, grazing on bacteria and fungi, and releasing plant-friendly nitrogen in the process.

how do we make soil healthy?

So, we know what soil we have, and how the perfect soil should function. But how does that relate to our garden? We cannot magically fill our soil with wondrous bacteria and fungi overnight, so we need to manage it thoughtfully to make it function well and support the plants we grow.

There are five main ways to make soil healthy:

1 Add regular quantities of high-quality, organic matter (see page 26), both worked into the soil surface and applied as a surface mulch. This will encourage populations of beneficial soil microbes to develop, protect the 'mineral' element of the soil from erosion and nutrient loss (leaching), and reduce water evaporation from the soil surface. A soil full of organic matter will be more consistent in structure, will hold water long enough for plants to drink and will bind any fertiliser we add.

2 Choose any other 'additives' carefully. The mantra 'What will it do to my soil?' should always be uttered before you add any fertiliser or pesticide. Pick the right products and they will work harmoniously with your soil flora and organic matter. The wrong additives could affect pH, salt levels and soil biology.

3 Minimise tillage (deep working of the soil). Although some traditional advice is to dig a soil 'open' in the winter and let the frost break it down, the more we discover about soil biology the less this seems right. Soils are not meant to be dug open and exposed. Deep digging and excessive rotavating undermines soil structure, creates compaction and threatens our beneficial soil flora. Most gardening techniques can be adapted to avoid deep tillage of the ground, most notably in vegetable growing where 'no-dig' and 'deep beds' are the most successful way to grow.

4 Minimise exposure of bare soil. In addition to mulching, the thoughtful gardener aims

for year-round coverage of the soil by plants, either through clever use of perennial planting or by sowing green manures. A bare soil is unnatural and undesirable, although it may be a strangely attractive sight to some!

5 Grow the right plants and plant combinations. Some plants exhaust the soil, while others bring unwanted diseases. The mantra is simple: growing the plants most appropriate to your garden is one of the simplest ways to maintain a healthy soil. Conversely, having a healthy soil is the simplest way to grow healthy, unfussy plants.

green manures

Armed with the knowledge that bare soil is undesirable and unsustainable, we must find ways to protect it or prevent it during fallow periods. This is why green manures are an indispensable tool in garden management.

Green manures are a group of plants that offer an umbrella against the damaging effects of wind, rain, sun and frost. The added appeal of green manures is that they offer extra bonus features, from providing nectar for bees to breaking up heavy soil.

As the table on page 24 illustrates, there are many choices for the gardener wishing to use green manures. Key considerations are timing and which extra benefits you want the green manure to provide.

Green manures for the winter

Many of us only have bare soil during the winter after we remove seasonal bedding or summer vegetables. The only green manures that will successfully germinate in autumn are grazing rye, tares (vetch) and field beans.

There is no denying the effectiveness of grazing rye for germinating and covering ground quickly, but it can look depressingly scruffy over a long, grey winter. However, one additional benefit is the fine, crumbly structure left behind by the fibrous roots of the rye and this could be of real use on a sticky, cloddy soil.

Field beans and tares will germinate and grow reliably as the chill of autumn sets in. Both are leguminous (*Fabaceae* family) and harness bacteria to 'fix' nitrogen (see page 18), which then acts as a fertiliser in future.

Green manures for the summer

Spring and summer green manures may not be in the ground for long. Lupin, mustard and phacelia can be sown in-between harvesting winter brassicas and sowing late fennel. Their role is to germinate quickly, cover the ground and out-compete weeds seeking to dominate. Lupins, being leguminous, also fix nitrogen. A leaf crop, which is able to harness this nutrient, such as spinach or cavalo nero, is the obvious thing to follow.

Phacelia is a wonderful fodder crop for bees and great to have in the ground when fruit trees and bushes are looking for pollinators. Mustard is the master of the fast turnaround and is the ideal thing for an actively managed vegetable garden.

Lupin makes an attractive green manure, offering soil protection against the elements during the summer months.

Fallowing

In some situations we may look to green manures to rescue failed soils. Excessively cultivated ground may be exhausted and, if only one crop has been grown on it, full of pests and diseases. It may be frustrating, but by allowing a green manure to grow for a whole summer on tired ground you may reap great benefit the following year.

green manures

NAME	BENEFITS	WHEN TO SOW	TIME IN GROUND
Alfalfa (*Medicago sativa*)	Fixes nitrogen, good subsoiler.	April–July	3–24 months
Buckwheat (*Fagopyrum esculentum*)	Fast to grow.	May–July	1–3 months
Field beans (*Vicia faba*)	Autumn germinating, fixes nitrogen, extremely hardy.	September–November	5–6 months
Lupin (*Lupinus angustifolius*)	Fixes nitrogen, good for light and acidic soils.	March–August	2–4 months
Mustards (*Brassica*)	Fast growing, high biomass, smothers weeds	March–August	1–2 months
Phacelia (*Phacelia tanacetifolia*)	Fast growth and decay, excellent nectar plant for bees.	March–August	1–3 months
Red clover (*Trifolium pratense*)	Fast growing, fixes nitrogen.	April–August	3–24 months
Italian rye grass (*Lolium multiflorum*)	Winter hardy, fast growing and germinating, smothers weeds.	April–September	6–8 months
Winter tares (*Vicia sativa*)	Winter hardy, late summer or early autumn germinating, fixes nitrogen.	August–October	2–8 months

As green manures are sown over large areas, it is useful to employ techniques that allow you to sow and turn in your green manure quickly and easily.

1 As soon your main crop is cleared, lightly fork over the soil to break up the surface.

2 Using a soil or landscape rake, make the area level. Use a cultivator or hoe to make drills (narrow trenches) in the soil.

3 Sow fairly roughly, adjusting spacing to suit the green manure species. For speed, it does not matter if you do not sow as consistently as you would for a food or flower crop – green manures generally do not reach full size anyway.

4 When it is time to turn the crop in, run over the plants with a lawnmower on its highest setting. If you have a small bed and want to save on carbon emissions, use old shears or a scythe. Leave all the cut foliage on the surface; this will add organic matter to the soil.

5 Depending on the size of your plot, turn the plants into the soil using a digging fork or a rotavator on its highest setting. If you are keen to add organic matter to the soil, put a thick layer over the cut stems and turn it in at the same time.

organic matter

Organic matter is a very broad term covering anything derived from living material, from dung to leaves. Gardeners have had a long and profound relationship with organic matter, harvesting waste to improve the productivity of crops and enhance the workability of soils. Every civilisation has used organic matter to improve its agriculture and horticulture, and the materials we use now have not changed much from those used thousands of years ago.

The main types of organic matter we use to improve our gardens are green-waste compost, manure, and pulverised bark and wood.

Green-waste compost

The move to reduce the amount of waste going to landfill in the UK has brought about the ubiquitous green bin for domestic garden waste. This is processed, generally to a very high standard, at municipal composting sites. Those used to a domestic compost set-up may be taken aback by the scale of this operation, with extraordinary volumes of compost being produced. The end product is normally fairly dark, uniform in size and weed-free.

Green-waste compost makes a good mulch and can be dug in as a soil improver. It can be fine in structure, so will not add as much bulk to your soil as rotted manure. You should take into account the tendency of green-waste compost to be alkaline and quite salty. If you have plants sensitive to pH, such as rhododendrons or heathers, or salt, such as young plants, it may be worth seeking out a different product.

Manure

One animal's waste is another's commodity. Animal manures have improved soil since the beginning of time and have wonderful properties. What distinguishes well-worked manures from other forms of organic matter is versatility. It adds organic bulk to poor soils, it works well as a mulch and its pH makes it useful for a wide variety of plant types.

Many of us have easy access to manure and for those who do not it is readily available and can be delivered loose or in bags. However, among this abundance, it is important to choose the right stuff, in the right condition.

Manure should be mixed with a little straw and allowed to compost before being used. Fresh manure has high levels of ammonia which scorches plants and therefore should be avoided. There is also scope for plant diseases such as *Phytophthora* to be present in the manure.

Another potential downfall for manures is their tendency to be weedy. Cold manures sitting around in farmyards attract weed seeds as they drift through the air. The tell-tale sign for badly processed manure is the vigorous 'flush' of weeds that appears shortly after delivery.

If manure is composted it stops smelling, ammonia levels decline and it becomes crumbly and easy to work. Weed-free 'composted manure' is a readily used term by suppliers and should be easy to find.

Pulverised bark and wood

Bark and wood chips come from two types of tree, pine and spruce, and can be a high-quality product from the right manufacturer. Bark chips have to be composted before they are used as a mulch or soil improver. As freshly made bark or wood chips break down, they do have the unfortunate habit of 'locking up' nitrogen so it becomes unavailable to plants. The next time you see an example of this form of mulching, look at the plants: they will be showing signs of nitrogen starvation, with leaves looking yellow around the edges.

Processed, composted bark chips should have excellent mulching potential, forming an attractive and effective barrier to the elements. Good manufacturers will be able | to tell you the pH and particle size and, as many pine-derived bark products have a low pH, this makes them suitable for mulching ericaceous plants such as azaleas, heathers and camellias.

Pine bark, when processed and composted, makes an excellent mulch.

making compost

Of course, we could just make organic matter ourselves: with some
careful planning, a bit of know-how and a little effort, composting
is easy and very rewarding.

Why should we compost?

Composting takes us closer to nature. In a perfect natural cycle, such
as in ancient woodland, the system is 'closed', meaning that no waste
is generated and nothing is imported from outside.

The management of organic matter, nutrients and waste in woodlands
has been perfected, seamlessly moving them from one form to another
to suit the season and requirements of the plants and animals within. A
leaf produces sugars and cools a tree down during the growing season.
When the leaves fall in autumn, they rot to provide organic matter for
the tree's roots.

Gardens sometimes bear little resemblance to closed systems,
as pesticides and fertilisers may be added to help plants grow
and 'waste' is removed in the form of weeds, leaves and prunings.
Successful composting is one way to help to 'close the loop', and
work towards a balanced soil that welcomes and nurtures plants.

It's not waste, it's a commodity

The making of good compost starts with a change in mentality. The
weeds, prunings, grass clippings and leaves generated by day-to-day
gardening should not be perceived as 'waste', an inconvenience
requiring time and effort to dispose of. Instead, simply view them
as 'building blocks' that are freely available to us to generate
a valuable and highly desirable garden product: compost.

Qualities of the best home-made compost

To recap, the best compost is a rich, dark, consistent form of organic matter, highly effective as a mulch and a great improver of poor, structureless soil. It will be weed and disease-free and easy to handle. The ability to produce such a wonderful, desirable product is within the grasp of many gardeners. The key to realising this ambition is a little space and an understanding of three key principles:

- Understanding the carbon-to-nitrogen ratio.
- Getting the moisture content correct.
- Knowing when and how to turn.

The thought of home composting can be off-putting to the novice gardener. The hard work you put into building your well-intentioned heaps is rewarded with bad smells and grey sludge or dry, dusty stuff that will never become useful to the garden. The key faults are always the same:

- There is too much freshly cut grass in it.
- The heap is too dry or too wet.
- Not enough oxygen has been allowed into the heap to aerate the compost.
- Through a lack of turning, no physical force has encouraged the compost to break down.

The perfect recipe

The perfect recipe for compost is: two parts carbon to one part nitrogen; 50 per cent moisture content throughout the life of the heap; and to be turned at least twice, although three times is desirable. All of this is preferably done in a 'hot' rather than a 'cold' system.

The difference between a hot and cold compost system is the difference between a heap that is made in one go and one that is added to a little at a time. Hot systems are undoubtedly more work and require more space – but achieve quicker, more trustworthy results.

Cold systems will produce good compost, but this is harder to guarantee and will take a lot longer. We will now look at how to make the best hot system and then consider ways to improve a cold one.

Browns to greens

We will start with the carbon-to-nitrogen ratio. There is no need to turn this into a chemistry lesson – in reality this is about achieving a balance of 'brown' waste to 'green':

    — **Brown waste** can include dry, fallen leaves, chipped or shredded branches, sawdust, straw, shredded cardboard or paper or old coir compost.

    — **Green waste** includes weeds, grass clippings, herbaceous plant material and animal manures.

When the balance of two parts brown to one part green is achieved in a 'hot' system, the perfect environment for a whole host of heat-loving bacteria and fungi is created. These microbial assistants quickly get to work on a freshly made heap, breaking down the brown and green waste, and releasing lots of heat as part of the process. The heat generated is extraordinary: 70–80°C within 24 hours. On a cold winter's day, it may appear as though a large kettle is boiling away under the tarpaulin.

This heat will sterilise the heap, killing the majority of weeds, seeds and diseases, as the table below shows.

If you know the temperatures your compost heap reliably reaches, you can make scientific judgements about what should and should not go in. Use a probe thermometer. The two weed seeds listed below can be easily destroyed in a well-made domestic compost heap, dispelling the myth that 'seeding weeds' should never go in.

The two diseases listed require more thought. An effective hot heap whose temperature is read on a weekly basis could be trusted to have *Phytophthora*-infected material added, especially as hot heaps tend to maintain heat for weeks or months at a time. If you are unsure about whether or not your heap will reach this temperature, do not add infected material.

temperature required to destroy garden weeds and diseases

WEED OR DISEASE	TEMPERATURE REQUIRED TO DESTROY WEED OR DISEASE	LENGTH OF TIME REQUIRED TO KILL WEED OR DISEASE
Annual meadow grass seeds	45°C	3 days
Prickly sow thistle seeds	45°C	3 days
Phytophthora	64–70°C	2–3 weeks
Mosaic virus	50–75°C	Can survive up to 6 weeks

Even the most committed of composters might look at the figures for mosaic virus with some caution. The top temperature of 75°C that is required to destroy it cannot always be guaranteed and its persistence – up to six weeks – means it could survive a good compost heap. For this reason, virus-infected material should be burnt or go through specialist processing systems, such as 'in-vessel' composting.

Moisture

Moisture is absolutely vital to a thriving compost heap. While plenty of plant material and a good carbon-to-nitrogen ratio are important, the primitive nature of the microbes involved means they cannot function in a dry world. To live, work and breathe they need to be surrounded by water.

Assessing the moisture content of your heap is best done with a 'squeeze' test. Pick up a handful of compost and squeeze. Does moisture seep out in-between your fingers? Too wet. Does the compost refuse to bind together in any way? Too dry.

A correct moisture level will feel like bagged compost from the garden centre. With hot compost, moisture is added throughout the construction of the heap; each layer could be doused with a hose or watering can, or a sprinkler could be set up to flick water gently on. Once 50 per cent moisture has been achieved, the heap should be covered to avoid it getting wetter in rain. It should be checked regularly, since if it goes dry at any stage then the compost will be compromised.

If your compost becomes too dry, simply water until it feels moist. If it becomes too wet, digging in some dry brown leaves, shredded cardboard or straw will help regain the moisture balance.

Turning compost

Why is it necessary to turn a compost heap? It is hard work and surely the compost will break down eventually, regardless of what we do? Turning the heap every three or four weeks is part of taking control of the composting process. When we turn compost we bring three key benefits to the system:

— The physical action of the fork digging in will break the compost down and stubborn lumps are bashed apart. Turning may be the difference between a heavy, lumpy compost and an even, consistent product with many purposes.

— By digging and moving the heap it is possible to see what is going on inside. A dry, dusty core may have formed in the heap, stopping further decomposition, or there may be lumps of grey mush to disperse. By dissembling and rebuilding the heap, serious issues like these can be sorted out by adding more water or dry matter (such as some handfuls of shredded cardboard).

— As the heap is opened up, a rush of oxygen is injected. This will kick-start any aerobic microbes left in the heap, allowing them to carry on with the 'hot', high-speed decomposition.

Making hot compost

To make hot compost effectively, a minimum of four bays or bins are required: one for storing green and brown waste; one for mixing the hot heap; and two for storing finished compost or turning into. The mixing bay should be 1½ times bigger than the storing bays. The minimum size of bay required to make hot compost may be smaller than you think: 1m³ (3ft³) has been scientifically proven to create a core of intense heat that is perfectly capable of sterilising the heap.

Use four bays in a hot-compost system. One for storing green and brown waste, one for mixing, and two for storing finished compost.

Basic bays can be made with fence posts and chicken wire or pallets. They will hold a large volume of heavy compost, so the stronger, the better. Using long fence posts with a third of their length dug into the soil will make a solid foundation. It is well worth looking at off-the-peg compost boxes or bays, as they will be designed with strength and ease of handling as priorities.

1 Make hot compost in one go, mixing thin layers of green and thick layers of brown waste. Bulky waste such as tree prunings, cordyline leaves or palm fronds are ideally chipped or shredded first. Water as you go, making sure each layer is moist, not dripping wet. Cover immediately to ensure that the heap gets no wetter or drier.

2 Your compost will get hot, quickly. Check the heap after a couple of days; there should be a hot core with plenty of steam bursting out. Invest in a probe thermometer that can penetrate into the heart of the heap. A good temperature is 60°C, but often 70–80°C can be achieved within a short time.

3 After a couple of weeks, or once the temperature has dropped by at least 10°C, turn the whole heap from the mixing bay into an empty storage bay. Turn again after a further two weeks, or once the temperature is down to 50°C.

Ideally the compost should be used once it is down to 30°C. It should look dark, crumbly and fairly consistent in structure. Make sure no weeds are germinating on it.

Cold compost

While hot composting is an exciting and thoroughly rewarding process, it may simply not be realistic in your garden. A lack of space, time or the correct ingredients can make hot compost hard to achieve. The main barrier may be how you garden, doing a few hours every weekend and creating a small amount of green or woody waste each time. This forms a 'cold' heap, so-called because a core of heat never forms. The reaction takes place on the outside layer, every time new waste is added.

The obvious disadvantage of a cold system is the lack of sterilisation. Because heat never generates consistently, weeds and diseases added to the compost heap over time will not break down and will breed in the compost. This limits the uses of cold compost, making it undesirable as a mulch or potting compost and relegating it to a deeply dug soil improver only. But cold compost is not bad, it is just different. The sheer power of nature will decompose any compost in time; it will just take a lot longer with a cold system.

Methods to improve a cold compost heap

There are some techniques that can help improve your heap and speed up the composting process:

— Turn. Turning a cold system, even two or three times a year will mix layers, add oxygen and give a chance to add extra materials. The physical action of fork against compost will also speed up the breakdown of the heap.

— Mix what you add. If you only add a little garden waste to the heap every week, make sure it's balanced. If you're cutting the grass, add some handfuls of shredded paper or dry brown leaves at the same time to allow 'good' composting to occur. This should also avoid the grass turning to grey sludge.

— Water the heap. A dry, cold heap that is turned and watered could spring into life and generate heat. Remember, 50 per cent moisture is ideal.

Cold compost heaps can be improved by turning.

Other garden composting systems

The open bays described on page 35 may not suit every garden but fortunately there are many alternatives on offer. Box and trench composting take up less space and there are ways to compost food, too.

Box composters

A bewildering array of vessels is available for neat, self-contained composting. Most of us are familiar with the 'dalek' issued by many local authorities. They are perfectly adequate for slow composting, providing they can be turned occasionally and the compost is not assumed to be weed-free. My biggest issue with this type of composter is the lack of access to the compost itself. Deep, narrow bins present a challenge if you are trying to turn regularly and although devices such as 'compost claws' are available, I am of the opinion that composting should be easy, not irritating.

A wide variety of clever alternatives address the ergonomic 'challenges' of the council composter, while retaining the attractive, compact dimensions. Earthmaker composters have a large volume – around 466 litres (102 gallons) and, crucially, three separate chambers for compost to move through. This allows three different ages of compost to be maturing at once, and the process of compost falling to the next layer replicates the benefits of turning. The Earthmaker is also designed to allow plenty of oxygen into the compost.

Greenline composters are well designed to take the strain out of composting. The key feature is easy access to the process, with a large lid that folds right back, and low, wide dimensions that make it easy to reach down to the bottom of the bin. Compost is easily removed from the base with large doors. Composters such as the Earthmaker and Greenline cost significantly more than council-supplied bins but they will reward anyone keen to develop their composting skills.

Trench composting

Trench composting may be the perfect solution if you cannot have a compost heap. Put simply, green gardening waste is thrown into a deep trench, which is then covered in soil. As the green waste breaks down it creates an organically rich zone, perfect for deep rooting crops, such as parsnips, that can penetrate far down into the soil.

1 Dig a trench one spade wide and one spade deep. It can run the length or depth of your vegetable bed.

2 Trench composting is a fairly slow process, so allow the trench several months to 'mature' before sowing or planting into it. Fill it with a layer of organic waste of any type: vegetable or fruit waste from the kitchen, weeds or herbaceous material. Add a layer of soil and start the next layer of organic waste. Cover with soil and leave.

3 With enough space you could create a rotation with trenches at two or three different stages and one always available for cultivation.

Composting food

Can food be turned into compost? As more councils introduce fortnightly landfill collections, it is time we took inspiration from Scandinavia and began to turn our food waste into compost.

Given the right conditions, anything of organic origin can be composted, and done correctly the process stops harmful quantities of methane (a major greenhouse gas produced from rotting food) from being released into the atmosphere.

The thought of composting waste food may be unpleasant and certainly if it is not done correctly, it will be. Picking the right method and equipment will ensure that food can become another 'organic asset' to your garden.

Uncooked vegetable and fruit waste can be incorporated into a compost heap, hot or cold, and be allowed to break down. A fairly general rule to follow being that anything green in colour will be nitrogen rich and anything brown will contain more carbon.

There are many food items that have traditionally been taboo when it comes to composting: meat and fish, cooked vegetables, bread, eggs and dairy products. While it may be undesirable (and unhygienic) to add these to an open compost heap, there are a range of specialist systems that offer an alternative to landfill.

Green cones and Green Johannas

Green cones break any food waste down using bacteria and heat from the sun. Placed in a warm, south-facing location, they thrive on small, regular additions of food waste but do not take garden waste. They can be slow to start, but once bacteria are present in effective quantities, they work extremely well. In a larger garden, where you have a garden compost system already in place, a green cone may be the perfect addition to add food composting to your repertoire. The only downside of cone systems is a lack of an end product (since waste is fully digested by the bacteria) and the work involved in installation. Cones are sited on a 60–70cm (24–28in) hole, which can take some digging and, preferably, gravel is incorporated into the bottom for drainage.

Cone composters use bacteria to break down food waste.

Green Johanna composters look similar to green cones but there are subtle differences. Green Johannas take garden waste (up to 30 per cent of the composter content), can be situated in shade and produce compost. If you have a small garden and want a 'do-it-all' unit to process modest volumes of garden waste too, then a Green Johanna may be the answer.

Bokashi and EM

Bokashi is a Japanese system for composting food, which again draws upon the efforts of beneficial bacteria to break down waste. EM stands for effective microbes (the bacteria that do the composting) and the two terms are interchangeable.

Bokashi bins sit in the kitchen and take regular additions of any food waste. They can be a little slow to get going and rely on regular additions of EM (which come in handy sachets or 1kg bags of bran) until the 'biology' of the system is working to perfection.

41

Tumblers

Tumblers also rely on bacteria to digest food, but here the addition of carbon, in the form of sawdust or wood pellets, creates a perfectly balanced environment for them to process any food waste. Superior tumblers have thick layers of insulation to retain heat, allowing the sort of temperatures that sterilise bacteria such as salmonella.

If you would like to try using tumblers for food waste, it is essential to purchase a decent probe thermometer (available from dedicated composting catalogues) to check the temperature on a regular basis. A temperature of 60°C will be enough to kill most of the problem bacteria and make the compost safe to handle (see page 32).

Add sawdust or wood pellets to help tumblers process food waste.

leaf mould

A curiously downbeat name for a wondrous product, leaf mould is excellent stuff. Dark, rich in humus and crumbly, leaf mould makes a terrific 'additive' when planting trees, a reliable, neutral base for potting compost and terrific mulch for ericaceous trees and shrubs. Simply composed of rotted leaves that are collected in autumn, there are several ways to accelerate and improve leaf mould:

— Leaf mould, like any 'dead' organic matter, will break down in time and become humus. Raking fallen leaves and stuffing them into black plastic sacks will allow this process to occur – but it may take years to break down properly and be let down by large 'reluctant rotters', such as plane, magnolia and laurel leaves.

— As with green-waste compost, adding moisture creates a more desirable environment for the microbes that break down organic matter. Unlike green-waste compost, there are no limits to how wet leaf mould can get, and by leaving it exposed to the elements we speed up decomposition.

— The principles of carbon-to-nitrogen ratio (see page 30) apply to leaf mould and, as fallen leaves are composed exclusively of carbon, the addition of green material has a dynamic effect. By moving fallen leaves on to grass and mowing them up, we add nitrogen (in the form of grass) and chop the leaves as they pass through the blades. Leaf piles processed in this manner can reach 70°C and break down in three to four months, meaning that an autumn's worth of fallen leaves can be used the following year.

compost tea

Compost tea is amazing stuff but, as with leaf mould, it suffers a bit of an image problem. Perhaps it is because of the name; it sounds a bit 'Heath Robinson', a sort of horticultural home brew surrounded by myth and rumour.

The reality could not be further from the truth. When made correctly, it is the single most potent 'biological' treatment for your garden.

Compost tea arose from commercial composting legislation. Large-scale farms and gardens are legally restricted in how much compost they can apply to their land every year. This is not a big deal to some, but to organic and biodynamic growers, this severely restricts their main technique for improving soil and creating plant health. But what if all the beneficial properties of compost could be converted into an easy-to-apply liquid form that could be diluted to cover large areas? What if this liquid form could be applied in bounteous volumes? I give you compost tea.

Compost tea has been produced on a large scale by chemical-free growers for many years and sophisticated technology and processes have evolved to ensure consistency and quality. The great news is that this professional approach is now available to domestic gardeners.

What is in compost tea?

Cast your mind back to my list of desirable organisms found in 'perfect' soil (see pages 14–19): beneficial bacteria and fungi, good nematodes and protozoa. They are all to be found in good compost tea along with humic acids (liquid organic matter) and some trace elements.

What are the benefits of compost tea?

The benefits to plants include improved growth and increased resistance to disease. Compost tea has been used on a large scale to completely eliminate fungicide use. Organic vineyards have virtually no chemicals available to combat powdery mildew (the key disease for vines) and producers, such as those at Laverstoke Park in Hampshire for example, are able to produce disease-free grapes thanks to regular compost tea applications. Professional nurseryman and women have succeeded in growing disease-prone ornamental plants such as lavender and heather without chemicals through compost tea applications.

If brewed to the highest standards, compost tea has other, diverse applications. Tired, compacted ground can be rebuilt using compost tea through the action of 'soil building' bacteria and fungi, plus it is also terrific for improving lawns.

How is compost tea made?

Compost tea is essentially just compost steeped in water, but there are several extra steps in the process to guarantee a high-quality product. The compost itself, the crucial ingredient, needs to be of the highest quality. This could obviously be from your heap and, if you follow best practice, there is no reason why this should not be the case. Brewing compost can also be bought and this has the advantage of containing guaranteed levels of beneficial microbes. Additives such as kelp, molasses and fish meal provide nutrition for the developing community of microbes and a mild, frost-free environment obviously helps.

Ideally compost tea is made in a dedicated brewing vessel that aerates the liquid (using a small pump) while it is brewing. Given the high volume of micro-organisms you are hoping to support, it is vital that there is a consistent oxygen supply. If you want to construct your own brewer, there should be little challenge in finding a deep plastic vessel, suitable for holding about 30 litres (6½ gallons) of liquid and an aquarium pump to add oxygen to the water. If you want to immerse yourself in the weird and wonderful world of YouTube, a great variety of demonstrations await online.

'Professional' compost-tea brewers produce a large volume of liquid that may be best shared between allotment holders or gardening clubs. A 20-litre (4-gallon) unit is ideal and can be bought from a professional horticultural supplier.

Making compost tea

1. Make sure the air temperature is a minimum of 20°C; any colder and you will struggle to breed good microbes. Fill the brewer with water and activate the pump. Small oxygen bubbles should be visible.

2. Many compost tea brewers recommend the water should be swirling before anything else is added. I have seen this done with a powerdrill and attachment, although you may just want to keep stirring by hand.

3. Add the dry nutrients and allow them to swirl for a few minutes so they are incorporated into the liquid.

4. The compost is put into a large mesh sack reminiscent of a giant tea bag. Add the bag and stir until it has absorbed water and is releasing liquid.

5. It is recommended that compost is brewed for a minimum of 48 hours, although some prefer 72.

6 When the tea is finished, dilute it down: one part tea to ten parts water. It can now be applied via a pressurised sprayer or watering can to pot plants, young glasshouse plants, lawns, shrubs and bedding.

7 The aim is to establish the microbes in compost tea around the plants you have treated and, for this reason, several applications may be required for an effective community to start thriving in the soil. If you have the time, fortnightly applications over a growing season should guarantee success.

Compost tea can be applied to a wide range of plants to improve growth and resistance to disease.

Water

Water is the second fundamental element that governs the life of plants. Many processes are driven by it, and the plant's very structure is built from it. Unsurprisingly, how we work with water decides whether our plants are successful or not.

death without water

It may not be the most attractive of images, but imagining your garden plants as big, wet balloons will help you to understand how they work.

As mentioned earlier (see page 9), plants can be composed of anything between 60 and 95 per cent water and the majority of living plant cells rely on being turgid (full of water) to maintain their structure and function properly. When the amount of water available to the plant decreases the turgor pressure (the ability to stay inflated) starts to decrease, putting the plant's systems under great stress.

Water does not just maintain structure. It also powers the 'transport system' within the plant that moves nutrients from the soil to cells, takes newly created sugars from leaves to be stored in roots and seeds, and removes waste products to be flushed out at the roots.

More primitive plants such as ferns and mosses cannot reproduce without water. Their ancient sexual system features separate male and female organs, living at either end of a small, specialised leaf (the gametophyte). In order for reproduction to occur successfully,

ferns and mosses thrive in a damp habitat because they need water to reproduce.

the male 'gametes' need to swim through a microscopic sea of water to reach the female side.

Water is therefore what most plants have based their evolution around. Myriad variations within the plant kingdom mean some plants last longer without water than others, but the fact remains that when water is unavailable, life becomes difficult, and then, sooner or later, impossible.

Water 'pressure'

Two physical effects put plants under water 'pressure': transpiration and evaporation:

Transpiration

Transpiration is an automatic, mechanical system plants use to cool down. Across a plant's leaves are tiny holes called pores, which open and close. When the plant is turgid, pores open fully and evaporating water vapour removes excess heat from the plant, not unlike sweating. When water is less available, the pores should close, reducing water loss. The problem comes on very hot days, when the plant is trying to lose heat and manage water loss simultaneously. If the plant is poorly adapted to the conditions, or growing in badly managed soil, the amount of water escaping through open pores may be out of control – a process known as evapo-transpiration. This phenomenon is seen when plants wilt in extreme heat, despite water being available in the soil.

Evaporation

Evaporation is the uncontrolled loss of water from soil and plant. Extreme heat will turn water into vapour and evaporate it away before plants have had the chance to use it, which is an extremely wasteful situation. Poorly maintained, un-mulched sandy soils are most likely to evaporate moisture and this should be a motivating factor when choosing the right plant for your soil type.

The movement of nutrients

Appearances can be deceptive. As a plant stands motionless in front of us, within, a mass of active, dynamic processes are taking place. In constant motion are nutrients drawn from the roots of the plant and sugars generated in the leaves. This traffic occurs within the 'veins' of the plant, known as phloem and the plant expends energy to power the process. As soon as water becomes at a premium, the exchange of nutrients and sugars is put under pressure.

how much water does a plant need?

How much water does a plant need? If you have chosen the right plant
for the conditions in your garden, the answer could be potentially none
at all. The worst thing to assume is that a plant will always need to be
watered, when in fact this approach can make the plant weak and more
prone to drought damage.

Soil and water are inextricably linked. If we know how much water our
soil holds and how long it takes to become dry, we make better decisions
about when to water. If we know how soils retain more moisture or
drain more freely, our decision making is even better informed.
Watering is a scientific process, like any other garden operation, and
by understanding more, we will use less water and grow better plants.

There are two key factors governing our approach to watering plants:
field capacity and permanent wilting point.

Field capacity

Field capacity is the maximum quantity of usable water a volume of soil
can hold. Field capacity happens after sustained rainfall and when excess
flood water has drained away: all soil pores are full of water and clay
soils are clinging on to water droplets. This is a perfect situation for a
garden: plants can draw water up readily, function normally and stress
levels are low, in stark contrast to permanent wilting point.

Permanent wilting point

Permanent wilting point signals death for plants. Field capacity has been
long passed: useful quantities of water have drained away and plants have
worked increasingly hard to bring water through their roots. Initial
wilting occurs when a lack of water reduces turgor pressure in the

cells and the plant can no longer keep itself fully inflated. Initial wilting is fairly superficial: given a renewed supply of water, the plant quickly regains its structure. However, a point occurs when a collapse in the tissues within the plant cannot be restored, permanent wilting point has been reached and the plant's systems shut down shortly afterwards.

The reality of gardening is that we spend most of our time working somewhere between flooded soil, field capacity and permanent wilting point. A perfect summer will see plenty of warm sunshine with just enough regular rainfall to maintain field capacity in the soil. When a less-than-ideal summer occurs, a good gardener will look deep into the soil to determine the best way to respond.

wise watering

Watering should never be done out of habit. This is an easy trap to fall into: we have not watered for a couple of days, the soil looks a bit dry and feels like it is time to water, but does the plant actually need it? We can literally kill our plants with excessive kindness and a thoughtful gardener will only water when plants really need it.

We occasionally have to play a dangerous game with our plants: is it serious wilting or just attention seeking? Will the plant recover as temperatures drop in the evening, or is it approaching permanent wilting point? Know your soil and your plant and the guessing stops.

At the height of a sunny spell, soil can look very dry. Scrape beneath the surface, around the plant roots and the story may be very different, with plenty of moist soil providing ample water. This extra analysis will delay the decision to water by days. Many herbaceous plants display wilting symptoms during hot weather and if we get to know their behaviour well, we can judge whether watering is really needed.

the mulch effect

In the battle against over-watering, mulching is an essential tool.
Is there a simpler, more effective way to improve our gardens than
mulching? A mulch can take many forms but its key purposes are
as follows:

— Minimising water evaporation from the soil by forming
a thick barrier over the top.

— Keeping plant roots cool by insulating them from direct
sunlight. This stops plants from going into 'heat-loss mode',
which could see them losing unnecessary water.

— Suppression of annual weed growth by literally smothering
any emerging seedlings.

Mulches are generally some sort of organic matter, with
well-made green-waste compost being the quickest and easiest
to apply. Commercially produced bark chips look really attractive
and are easy to spread but can be expensive. As they rot down
they form an effective organic layer in the soil.

Some more esoteric mulches include crushed glass, recycled
vinyl records and composted straw, but they all play the same
fundamental role of creating a protective layer between the air
and the soil.

When to mulch

If you can, mulch should be applied twice a year, namely mid-spring and
late summer or early autumn, when the soil is moist and neither frozen
nor waterlogged.

The spring application will catch out weed seedlings just when they are planning to emerge and will insulate plant roots as the air temperature starts to rise.

The late summer application reduces stress on plants as they start to enter dormancy, protecting the soil from stormy, frosty autumn and winter weather. It will also inhibit the irritating weed germination that can occur in milder spells of late winter or early spring.

the dangers of over-watering

Plants respond rapidly to their environment. If there is regular, plentiful water the plant will 'over-grow', forming a shape bloated on this excess. Roots that feel no need to search deep for water will rise to the surface and sit waiting for the next irrigation. This situation may not appear a problem until a hosepipe ban or drought order appears, or the temperature rises to a point where plants cannot control evaporation.

There is now little water available, so what does the plant do? The bloated structure still needs water to stay inflated and will wilt rapidly and dangerously as the garden dries up. The lazy roots sitting on the surface are now extremely prone to drying out and dangerous evaporation and have no ability to search deep in the soil, where the last of the water most likely still remains. In short, our spoilt, over-watered plants are in trouble.

The situation described above may seem melodramatic – but this is why watering needs to be treated as scientifically as possible.

Here are a few basic rules about what does and does not need water in the garden:

Lawns: do not need to be watered. When establishing a young lawn, take the opportunity to get it right by creating the right growing medium for grass (see page 172). Follow up this good work by watering extremely sparingly to get grass seedlings established.

After this, never water again – your grass will become tough and more deep-rooted for it. In intense droughts, the sight of a lawn turning brown can be alarming, but this is nothing more than a defence mechanism; a healthy lawn goes into a form of summer dormancy but will quickly recover once rain returns.

Trees and shrubs: should only be watered when establishing and after that, only when they are in danger of dying (in an intense drought situation). The vast majority of mature trees will have roots capable of tapping into the water table, and are sophisticated enough to manage their water uptake in extreme heat by dropping leaves. If your established shrubs need regular summer watering they may not be right for your garden, or the roots have never left the surface of the soil, perhaps because of over-watering early on.

It is vital that young trees and shrubs survive their first growing season. No matter how well a tree or shrub is grown, the process of removing from a pot, or lifting from bare ground, will cause roots stress and damage. If the plant can quietly settle in the soil, it develops a strong, active root system that can forage deep in the soil, becoming self-sufficient. September plantings help, giving the young plant a couple of months to establish in non-stressful conditions before winter so they are ready to grow in spring.

Herbaceous perennials: are tough, needing very little help after their first few months in the ground. The big challenge comes when designing and managing mixed herbaceous borders. By its very nature, the mixed border might mix bog plants and Mediterranean plants, annuals and roses, and this means a vast array of different watering regimes may be required.

Although some compromise may be needed, mixed borders can be redesigned for efficient watering. Placing plant groups according to their desire for water will allow you to irrigate specific sections only, leaving dry-climate plants unwatered. It may sound like design heresy to suggest planting on the basis of water requirements, rather than colour, form or height, but the sheer variety of plants available allows creative flair to be expressed easily.

Annuals: are traditionally thought of as the big consumers. Pesticides, fertiliser and water are all required in regular quantities for garden bedding to rival what we see planted in municipal town displays. Or are they? With a thoughtful, scientific approach to the state of the soil and the needs of our plants, bedding can be grown with very little need for water.

Well-designed borders, such as this herbaceous border featuring geranium and iris, need little water.

A new approach to watering bedding plants

My own experience of controlling how little water annuals
need comes from the large summer borders at Nymans in
Sussex. Planted with 6,500 annuals, they have the potential
to consume vast amounts of water, fertiliser and pesticides.

In 2006 we were confronted with a significant drought
and the need to provide a spectacular display for
visitors. Luckily this situation coincided with a
study into the drought tolerance of bedding

petunias, a major constituent of the summer borders. The study asked a commercial nursery to water four batches of petunias in different ways. Batch 1 received regular watering, batch 2 half as much as batch 1, batch 3 a quarter the amount of batch 1 and batch 4 was left to fend for itself.

Which group did best?

Unsurprisingly, batch 4 was a sad sight, but the real revelation came with batches 2 and 3. Instead of struggling with less water than normal, they were green, healthy and full of flower and buds. Batch 2 was virtually the same size as batch 1, albeit with a 'leaner', wiry growth habit, and although batch 3 was smaller, it bore only a few less flowers than the conventionally watered plants.

Watering experiments found that plants can adjust to different watering regimes.

Batch 1   Batch 2   Batch 3   Batch 4

The conclusion was obvious: annual plants can thrive on a number of different watering regimes and adjust how they grow accordingly. Minimal watering results in a lean framework for the plant; indulgent watering will produce a 'big, wet, balloon' as the plant gorges on plentiful water.

We adapted this piece of science to the summer borders at Nymans. Calculating how often we watered in the past, we reduced it by a quarter and dug plenty of good-quality, moisture-retaining compost into the soil.

Days, then weeks would go by without watering. How long could we leave it before the next irrigation? Was the soil dry now? It looked so on the surface, only to find moisture when we scraped down to the plant's roots. During the drought of 2006, we only watered our annual bedding four times between May and October, and these principles can be applied in any garden.

How will this work in my garden?
Buy your bedding when it is small and still has plenty of growing to do. Plant it into really well-conditioned soil and hide your watering can. Let the plants adapt to their environment. If there is not much water they will produce deep roots and limit how much lush, green growth they make. What they will give you is flowers. Annual bedding is quite simply programmed to flower and a low-watering regime will not deter it.

harvesting water

Water is sometimes abundant, at other times stressfully elusive. By harvesting rainwater, we give ourselves access to a free commodity, which will always be useful to the garden.

Why should we collect water?

In the midst of a hosepipe ban, we may look back wistfully at the winter that has just passed and think of all the rain that fell on and then drained through, our garden.

In a temperate country such as the UK, it often feels as if collecting rainwater is unnecessary, given how much rain we often get. Looking more closely at the facts should discourage any complacency. Some parts of the UK, particularly in the east, have more in common with the Mediterranean basin when it comes to rainfall, and spend significant parts of the year on a drought footing. Other areas receive lots of rain but often as violent 'storm events', with high volumes of water landing quickly and then washing away before it can be absorbed by the soil or used by plants.

Possibly of most significance is how quickly the threat of drought can raise its head. Many typical British gardens need regular water to thrive due to the plants grown in them, and it only takes a couple of weeks of dry weather to get us twitchy, checking the weather forecast for the first hint of showers. Parts of the country are so densely populated that there is not enough water to go round for humans and plants once we get into drought and, before we know it, hosepipe bans and drought orders threaten to ruin our summer crops and displays. Given all of this, surely we should explore ways to store all that rain that lands on our garden at certain times of the year?

Harvesting rain and waste water

There are two types of water we can harvest: rain and waste. Rain is best caught with guttering; either on a house or garden building where it can be collected in that most humble of vessels, the water butt.

Waste water is harder to catch, but when the amount that washes off paths, patios and driveways is taken into account, there should be a reasonable incentive.

Water butts collect up to 200 litres (44 gallons) of water and will steadily fill up a watering can via a small tap, although small submersible pumps are quicker. Their greatest drawback is that they are full of water during wet periods and quickly empty, leaving little more than green sludge when it gets hot and dry.

The algae and bacteria that build up in water butts can smell fairly unhealthy and may occasionally contain serious plant diseases. Therefore, a regime for keeping the water fresh and stimulated is useful. Several branded products with names such as Water Clear or Refresh Water Cleaner are available and reduce the algal growth without being toxic. A healthy population of mosquito larvae or water lice also maintain clearer water. The other option is to top up from the mains if the water butt levels drop below a certain level (below 40 per cent, for example).

Collecting on a bigger scale

Ambitions go beyond mere water butts, when some exciting options are available. Building a new drive or patio? Why not bury a 1,000-litre (220-gallon) tank underneath? The right investment will buy a tough plastic tank, contoured to fit any number of awkward spaces, with enough litreage to allow mains-free watering throughout a dry summer. Tanks can be fitted with integrated pumps to allow easy irrigation.

Larger above-ground tanks mark a step up from water butts and have been designed with a variety of garden spaces in mind. They provide scope for hundreds of litres to be stored.

Collecting waste water

During a wet spell, many thousands of litres of water run through and out of our gardens. The first, most straightforward step is to collect rain. The next progression is to 'close the loop' and re-use the water that runs off the ground too. The best way to catch run-off water is to ensure it ends up in a drain or gulley that can handle the volumes of water generated in a storm. The gulley or drain could then run to a tank or pond to be used when the weather gets drier.

An example of a water run-off collection system

— Use gravity and impermeable surfaces to your advantage. Does your patio slope? Does water run out of your glasshouse door?

— Simple, open drains can be used to collect run-off water. Alternatively, lots of hardware shops and websites sell a product known as Garage Drain, which is perfect for catching water.

— Unless you have lots of money to spend on pumps, use gravity to collect your water. Using PVC drainage pipe (110-mm pipe is perfect), run water downhill to a buried collection tank, preferably with a minimum capacity of 1,000 litres (220 gallons). Burying a tank of this size is best done by reputable landscape or building contractors. They will discuss the limitations of your site and suggest a wide, shallow tank or a deep 'bottle' type tank depending on how deep they can dig. They should also make provision for any excess water to overflow to a soak-away drain.

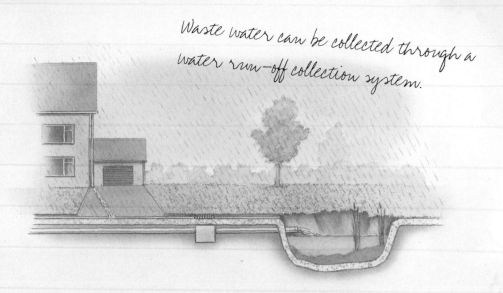

Waste water can be collected through a water run-off collection system.

— A submersible pump is the best way to draw water out of a buried tank. This could be used to water the garden directly or to fill water butts and be used later.

Managing storm water

While much is made of the hotter, drier summers that will result from climate change, it is the increasingly violent spells of rain that could hold a greater threat. Traditional drains are built around steady, persistent rain, not intense 'storm episodes' and gardens, pavements and roads can quickly become saturated in a downpour, leading to damaging flooding.

We are starting to grasp the impact of storm water in the UK. New legislation, known as Sustainable Urban Drainage Systems (SUDS), ensures that new developments deal with water in a sustainable way, reducing the threat of storms and using waste water more. A typical example of SUDS in practice is legislation outlawing the concreting over of front gardens to make car parks, due to the volume of flood water that is generated from a large, flat, impermeable surface. There is much we can do when planning our gardens to catch flood water and allow it to drain away gradually.

Permeable materials

Many landscaping materials will drain gradually, rather than letting water flow off their surface. Plastic grids are readily available from builders' merchants and larger garden centres and form 'cells' in a network of grids laid over a newly developed area. The cells can be filled with soil, gravel or other aggregates and the design of the cells allows slow, controlled drainage to the soil below.

Permeable landscaping materials

When working with hard landscaping surfaces, such as patios and paths, there are plenty of permeable materials to choose from.

— There are lots of products available to professionals and amateurs to construct permeable surfaces. Coming with names such as Permeable Eco Paving or Net Pave, they are essentially plastic grids that can be filled with soil, turf or gravel and fitted together to make driveways or paths. If your area is going to bear significant weight, such as for car parking, it is well worth seeking the advice of a builder.

— When creating a new 'hard' area such as a path, parking space or patio, work with level ground and create a foundation with a coarse aggregate such as Type 1 stone (MOT) or scalpings. Even when compacted, this type of material will still allow water to percolate.

— Paving units lock together and, providing they are laid on to level ground, should be easy to install. Retain the network of paving units around the outside with some more Type 1 stone or dry mixed concrete. Depending on the size of the unit, any number of different materials can be used to fill them in. Ensure the material is not packed too hard to ensure water can drain through slowly.

Swales

Another technique being used more in the light of SUDS legislation, swales are essentially long ditches capable of swallowing significant volumes of storm water, and are often filled with bog plants.

Swales should be located wherever there is the danger of rapid run-off occurring and be large enough to catch and hold the volume of water the area produces. Alternatively, a system of swales could be dug, with each catching a certain amount of overflow. Once held in a swale, water can slowly percolate away.

Swales can collect storm and other run-off water and are a wonderful habitat for bog plants.

Protecting plants

Once we understand what a plant requires from its environment to be healthy, this should actively influence the choices we make when developing our garden. It is now time to look at plants themselves and to understand how they work and the threats to their health and well-being.

Choosing the right plants for your garden can mean the difference between joy and despair, so I will now look at some typically challenging garden habitats and suggest plants that would be suitable for each environment.

the healthy plant

The typical plant needs, in no particular order, the following things: light, water and nutrients. It also needs to be free of diseases and major pest attacks.

A healthy plant avoids water stress by being well adapted (see page 51). Every species also has its own light requirements, from intense sun to deep shade and it is up to us to select the right plant for the right place in the garden. All the nutrients a plant needs are available from the perfect soil and, if they are not, we need to decide what is missing and how to rectify an imbalance.

The healthy plant will encounter diseases but will fight them off, either by itself or with a little help from us. We need to keep an eye on pests and intervene when necessary, but the balanced nature of the garden will help to regulate numbers.

diseases

What is a disease?

Plants get ill, just like humans. Pathogens such as viruses, bacteria and fungi are always looking for plants to attack and many of them have specific garden favourites. Plant diseases affect gardeners in different ways. For some, the unpleasant sight of mottled or distorted foliage detracts from our perfect display; for others, there would be a impact on our finances or subsistence if we lose significant food crops. Beloved trees and shrubs can be lost if an aggressive disease strikes, which can be a distressing experience and, on a commercial scale, nurseries can be put out of business in worst-case scenarios.

Do plants have to get ill?

During a difficult growing season, it can feel like plants are destined to become ill, that it is somehow fated. If we eat well and look after ourselves, we can reduce our chances of getting ill and recover more quickly if we do, and for plants it is no different.

A healthy plant, growing in healthy soil, is in balance with its surroundings and has a fully functioning immune system. Diseases struggle to establish in the soil around the plant due to the healthy biology present and the plant itself can combat the attack of fungi, viruses and bacteria. By following the guidance for improving soil in this book (see page 20), a significant step will be taken towards reducing disease levels in the garden.

How to manage disease in the garden

— Employ every method available to create healthy, biologically active soil.
— Choose disease-resistant plants.
— Buy 'clean', disease-free stock from nurseries to bring into the garden.
— Maintain healthy plants through pruning, addressing deficiencies and timely propagation.

Controlling and eliminating diseases

Sometimes, there is nothing that can be done. The need to grow plants for sentimental or historic reasons, or physical factors within our gardens means that, despite our best efforts, diseases appear.

At this juncture, the thoughtful gardener does not panic and spray the nastiest fungicide *ad nauseam*. Instead, a series of clever measures can manage or eliminate plant diseases without affecting the deeper balance and rhythms within the garden.

cultural controls

Manipulate conditions to make it harder for disease to thrive. This could be by changing ventilation, humidity, temperature, drainage or moisture retention. Crop rotation is a significant cultural method to reduce disease levels for vegetable gardeners, while for rose enthusiasts pruning effectively manipulates airflow around the plant.

Venting your glasshouse

— If you have side and top vents, open these together, especially first thing in the morning when glasshouses tend be full of damp air. If you have the luxury of thermostatically controlled heating, turn this up for a brief period to encourage the damp air to rise out of the top vent.

— Fit vents with simple, automatic openers that respond to a rise in temperature. This will stop excess humidity and potentially damaging heat levels forming.

— Vents can be retro-fitted to many glasshouses, with simple units available from the more serious catalogues.

— If you have a simple polythene or glass unit to raise tender plants in, always check humidity levels while young seedlings are growing. This can be done either by feel or a simple, hand-held hygrometer.

Effective ventilation reduces disease in glasshouses.

Pruning

To improve cultural conditions for shrubs such as roses, spend some time pruning them. For the purposes of this book, we will focus solely on pruning as a means for reducing disease and creating healthier plants. If you want to learn more about pruning, you will find more information in Further Reading (see page 188).

Consider the ideal conditions for blackspot, rust, downy and powdery mildew to breed. All of these diseases thrive in still air and a congested old rose constitutes the perfect environment for them. Pruning is the way to clarify the shape, remove disease-prone material and create a much-needed flow of fresh air through the centre of the plant.

Pruning roses

Pruning is plant specific and it pays to research before you brandish your secateurs. In general, all roses can be thinned and opened out in the late winter (a mild day in late February is perfect), but very hard pruning should be reserved for vigorous modern hybrid tea and floribunda roses. Older types of roses should be reduced more gently and prudently.

1 All pruning cuts should be made with clean, sharp secateurs that are adjusted to be not too tight or loose. Cuts should be made around 2–3mm above a bud with a slope to direct rainwater away from the open wound.

2 Crossing growth rubs together in the wind, making 'sores' that are prone to infection. The crossing point also acts as a 'bridge' for diseases and pests to move along. For these reasons, remove all crossing growth, back to a bud.

3 The three Ds – dead, diseased and damaged – will only make your plant less healthy. Remove them, cutting back to the first healthy bud you find.

4 Growth thinner than a pencil will not bear good flower and could undermine the plant by splitting later on, so remove it.

5 Now stand back and look at your rose. Is the centre of the plant open? Can you feel the breeze flowing through it? The next step is to simplify the structure with all growth parallel and facing out. Cut anything pointing towards the centre of the plant back to a strong, outward-facing pink bud. Step back after each cut to take in the overall shape of the plant. Hold your hand or a piece of card in front of the stem you want to remove. Often what feels like a big incision improves the appearance of the plant enormously.

Pruning roses reduces disease and creates healthier plants.

6 If your rose is modern and vigorous, you can remove up to 70 per cent of the previous year's growth. If your rose is of a gentler persuasion, remove 20–30 per cent; any less and the plant will be seriously floppy by the end of the summer; go harder and it will respond by producing wild, scruffy tendrils that will not produce much flower.

71

Crop rotation

Vegetable diseases love repetition. Most of the major garden pathogens naturally associate with one of the significant food crop families and, given the same host year-in, year-out, bacteria and fungi establish strong, thriving communities that can quickly bring young, newly planted vegetables to their knees. Some of the worst examples of this are blight in potatoes, club root in cabbages and mosaic viruses in tomatoes.

The advantage of vegetable diseases specialising in certain families is that by rotating the plant families in each vegetable bed, we take away the disease's only reason for existing. Unable to thrive on a different plant family, the pathogen's strength is greatly diminished and, if rotations are timed correctly, by the time the original plant family returns the disease levels in the bed are negligible.

With a four-bed system it will make sense to change the plant family every year, so the plant family should not return to the original bed for at least four years. There are four main plant families involved in vegetable growing:

Fennel can be grown as part of a rotation system.

> **Solanaceae:** tomatoes, peppers, potatoes, physalis
> **Cruciferae:** cabbages, rocket, sprouts, cavalo nero, broccoli, radish
> **Apiaceae:** parsnips, carrots, celeriac, fennel
> **Asteraceae:** sunflowers, lettuce, artichokes, salsify

It is relatively easy to keep vegetable beds themed around these plant families. Long-term record keeping will help you keep track of the rotation.

biological controls

Products are available that control or eliminate disease using biological agents, either directly attacking the pathogen or by boosting plant health to increase immunity.

Bottled bacteria

Fungicides are highly effective products for controlling many fungal diseases and deliver disease-free glasshouses and gardens, but they will not feature in this book.

This has nothing to do with being organic; indeed, several fungicides such as sulphur are approved for organic use. In this book I want to showcase a different way of managing a garden; a biological one.

As we have already seen, a wild soil is inhabited by a multitude of bacteria, fungi, nematodes and protozoa, many of whom are plant allies. Through a combination of mopping up waste starches, out-competing 'nasty' microbes and making the plants' roots function more efficiently, it is simply harder for diseases to thrive.

Many of the recent developments in commercial horticulture have focused on isolating and bottling some of these allies for gardeners to buy along with their canes and compost. Although these allies can be found in good compost and compost tea, the specific action of one microbe means there is value in isolating it and selling separately.

Bacillus subtilis (sold under the brand names Revive and Serenade) has long been identified as a key player in any healthy soil-plant relationship. It has now been thoroughly tested and approved as a control for disease fungi, and this is a huge development for the thoughtful gardener.

The introduction of *Bacillus* has a direct effect on fungi already present in the plant or soil and also acts as an inoculant, 'vaccinating' seedlings against disease. It offers the opportunity to eliminate chemical fungicides from our growing. It is best used at three different stages:

Using *Bacillus* to control disease

1 When preparing your seed trays, fill with compost and firm as normal. Then water the seed tray with *Bacillus*, using a flowing motion with the watering can over the tray. Make sure you do not over-water: the compost will only be able to hold on to some of the many beneficial bacteria. The young seedlings will quickly form an association with the *Bacillus* breeding in the compost.

2 Pricking out is a stressful process for plants. No matter how carefully done, there will be root damage to the seedlings as they are prised out. This root damage can make the plant vulnerable. Water *Bacillus* on to a freshly pricked-out plant and again once it has clearly started to grow to reduce stress.

3 *Bacillus* can be used out in the garden. Disease-prone plants such as *Antirrhinums* show early symptoms of rust infection in the form of small pustules on the leaf. *Bacillus* can be applied at this stage and several regular doses give *Antirrhinums* a chance of fighting back. However, the gentle, symbiotic way that *Bacillus* works means it will struggle to rescue a heavily diseased plant.

Milk

Milk controls a variety of fungal diseases. It contains fungicidal enzymes and potassium phosphate to stimulate an immune response in plants.

1 Pick the right day: it should be warm but not hot, with no rain forecast.

2 Mix one part full-fat, organic milk with ten parts of water. Add a couple of drops of sunflower oil and biodegradable washing-up liquid to emulsify the solution and make it stick to the foliage.

3 Spray on to the foliage until drips form on the edge of the leaf. Spray both sides of the leaf. A pressurised sprayer would be a good investment, making the job quick and effective.

4 Milk sprays are best done regularly. Start as soon as buds open and apply every fortnight until autumn.

Spraying plants with milk prevents fungal disease.

Garlic

Garlic is a highly effective and diverse tool for managing a healthy garden. Approved for use in commercial organic gardening, it is fungicidal, insecticidal and contains some minor nutrients, such as selenium. Regular applications of garlic to disease- and pest-prone plants (such as roses) can give you control over the whole growing season.

Garlic that has been prepared for garden use comes in two forms, granular and liquid. The liquid is diluted down following label guidance and applied liberally to affected plants. It works by contact action so you need to make sure it has covered the affliction you are trying to remove. Granules can be dug into unhealthy soil or applied around disease-prone plants.

A word of caution: although it is natural, garlic will have a negative effect on any beneficial fungi you are trying to build in the soil. If you are using compost tea or *Bacillus subtilis* culture, make sure you leave some time before you apply garlic. You should leave at least two weeks between applications of compost tea or *Bacillus subtilis* and garlic.

garlic can be applied to plants or dug into soil to protect plants from disease.

the main diseases of ornamental plants

The main diseases affecting ornamental garden plants are: damping off, powdery and downy mildew, rust, blackspot and honey fungus. On the following pages you will find advice on how to deal with them.

Fruit and vegetables are most threatened by club root, blight, mosaic virus, canker and leaf curl. See pages 84–90 for how to control diseases affecting fruit and vegetables.

Damping off

The collective term applied to a group of pathogenic fungi, damping off is a particularly cruel disease, striking at weak, defenceless seedlings, generally in glasshouses. The size and vigour of the victims means only a short time between the first symptoms of the disease and death, making it hard for a gardener to respond quickly.

The fungi that cause damping off are around us in the 'rain' of tiny fungal spores. When they find a host (such as seedlings) they colonise root space or the young tip of the seedling. The speed of the fungi's growth is devastating to the plant. Sugars are removed to feed its requirements and eventually plant tissue is destroyed. The infected seedling becomes covered in fungal fruiting bodies and the seedling's roots are consumed.

Control

Damping off can be restricted and even eliminated by employing cultural and biological control measures. Good glasshouse hygiene is crucial. Never allow piles of leaves, weeds or rotting plant material to build up inside. Decaying organic matter breeds disease spores and will undermine any other methods of disease prevention. Be careful when handling young plants: small rips or tears in the plant tissue are perfect

77

entry points for fungal spores. When taking cuttings, ensure the smallest possible scars are made when leaves are removed and stems cut.

Damping off fungi thrive in still, damp conditions and by venting a glasshouse, the favourite habitat for damping off fungi is removed. Cool, not cold glasshouses make for strong, healthy young plants and start the process of hardening-off (making the plant hardy for outside conditions).

Use of *Bacillus subtilis* throughout the propagation process will severely reduce the threat of damping off fungi.

Powdery mildew

Powdery mildew is symptomatic of long, dry spells during the summer. For this reason, it is associated with August and early September. This unfortunately coincides with the garden starting to slide into autumn and dry, dusty foliage adds to the sense of decline.

Powdery mildew is always seen on the top side of leaves as a powdery white dust and affects a wide range of plants. Although some infection is inevitable during a dry summer, powdery mildew is often a fairly mild affliction, with a cosmetic impact such as leaves losing their gloss and some of their colour. In a prolonged dry spell, powdery mildew is a more serious threat, causing leaf drop and disfiguring roses. In these situations, a response is required quickly, due to the gentle nature of the remedies used by the thoughtful gardener.

Control

Review your garden at the end of the summer. Walking round, notice what has succumbed to powdery mildew. Is it the same plants as last year? Has the summer been excessively dry? If so, you could excuse some plants for displaying symptoms. However, if there have been regular spells of rainfall and certain plants appear to be infested, what should be done?

Should that plant be in your garden at all? If it is struggling for moisture and getting stressed enough for powdery mildew to take hold, the plant is not ecologically adapted to the garden. *Monarda* (bergamot) is prone to powdery mildew and often ends the summer looking extremely unattractive. Originating from the damp prairies of North America, *Monarda* cultivars struggle in many UK gardens and the question 'Is it worth it?' should definitely be asked.

Although powdery mildew is a late-season disease, proactive prevention begins as soon as the plant is in active growth. Cultural controls include the regular removal of weeds that may bear spores around the plant and watering foliage occasionally during dry periods.

Spraying regularly with milk will inhibit the development of powdery mildew during the course of the summer so the disease becomes weak and unable to dominate the plant late in the season.

Downy mildew

In contrast to powdery mildew, downy mildew thrives in damp, warm conditions and appears during wet summers, when humidity levels peak. It is easily recognised by little piles of grey mould thickly covering the underside of the leaf. The topside turns blotchy yellow when the disease really takes hold.

Control

As downy mildew tends to be less endemic to gardens, it is easier to justify an intervention. Prompt removal of infected foliage is essential and this can be burned or composted, depending on how hot your heap gets (see page 32).

The earliest symptoms of downy mildew are very small pustules or discoloured patches forming on the topside of the leaf. At this stage, ensure the best airflow around the plant. Is it surrounded by other shrubs? Is the plant itself congested? If you can, improve the plant's ventilation, then move on to spraying to cure the plant before the disease takes full hold.

Providing the disease is still at an early stage, weekly applications of *Bacillis subtilis* or garlic may allow the plant to fight back against infection. The beneficial bacteria will try to out-compete the fungus causing downy mildew, while improving the efficiency of the plant's root system. Alternate applications of garlic will kill fungal spores – you should leave at least two weeks between applications of *Bacillis subtilis* and garlic.

Rust and blackspot

Rust and blackspot are the two biggest threats to roses, although rust can also disfigure flowering shrubs such as *Mahonia*. Both diseases are fungal and extremely common.

As with powdery mildew, rust and blackspot can become 'indigenous' to prone plants and it is vital to assume that these two diseases will appear as the growing season progresses. If anything, rust and particularly blackspot are more serious than powdery mildew. Left unchecked, leaves become heavily distorted and eventually completely black with disease and plants will often end the summer without any leaves left.

Control

Both diseases breed prolifically through microscopic bodies called spores. As soon as either disease is visible on the leaves of plants, there will be literally billions of spores in close proximity, waiting to infect fresh foliage.

The cultural control for blackspot and rust is spore removal. Look around the base of the infected plants: are there piles of leaves? Or weeds? These could be harbouring spores and should be cleared away and hot composted or burnt.

Roses, in particular, should have clear space around them, with nothing but a thick layer of mulch. This is not to the taste of garden romantics who cherish the sight of *Geranium* and *Nepeta* (catmint) growing among their rose stems but the reduction in disease levels would justify this aesthetic compromise. Any pruning should ensure an open, healthy shape for a bush that permits good airflow.

Spray garlic for disease control. Start applying as soon as leaf buds open (in a mild spring this could be as early as mid-March) and apply every fortnight. As an alternative, monthly foliar feeds using a seaweed fertiliser (such as Maxicrop) will nourish the rose as it flowers.

Why not just spray with a fungicide? There is no doubt that fungicides are highly effective against rust and blackspot, but you need to look beyond the end result (clean roses). Using a chemical fungicide regularly will build salt levels in your soil, affecting the chemical balance and undermining the beneficial soil flora.

Honey fungus

Although the name honey fungus is associated with death, it is important to remember that mature trees live with it for decades and it lives in most gardens.

Increased stress and a compromised immune system tip the balance and allow honey fungus to take hold and shut down trees. When honey fungus is rampant, it can cause waves of destruction, killing hedges, young trees and shrubs.

An early sign of honey fungus is the plant wilting, in spite of moist soil. At this stage the strong 'bootlaces' or rhizomorphs of honey fungus are breaking down the plant's root system, stopping it from drinking. Foliage turns from green to brown as the plant's systems are shut down and death follows soon after. In the autumn, the tell-tale honey fungus fruiting bodies appear; golden coloured with a pleasant honey scent and a distinctive frill around the top of the stalk.

Control

How do you control the world's largest organism (see page 16)? Keep your garden plants as healthy and stress-free as possible. Thick layers of mulch, applied when the soil is moist, keep roots cool and reduce evaporation (see page 53).

One of the quickest ways to bring about decline in a tree is by compacting the fine, living roots near the surface, and regular human traffic is enough to do this. Placing a large 'tree circle' of good organic matter deters compaction and encourages healthy roots. Use of mycorrhizal conditioners and fertilisers can maintain good health in woody plants, especially when they are young, but will not reverse serious infection.

It is hard to accept, but when a mature tree is in the final throes of a honey fungus infection, it is time to be pragmatic and get the tree felled professionally before it becomes a hazard. Removing all of the tree and grinding out the stump is wise, as the bootlaces linger in the soil, feeding off any wood remaining. Opinion is divided over replanting with another tree and it should not be assumed that honey fungus will immediately devour a strong young specimen with lots of living roots.

If your hedge or new planting of lavender has been destroyed (often looking as if someone has set fire to them), it should be assumed that the honey fungus is in an agitated, rampant state. It may be prudent to replant with herbaceous material (an exciting opportunity to experiment?) or a woody plant not favoured by the disease (the Royal Horticultural Society produce a list of suitable species).

fruit and vegetable diseases

It is easy to get emotional about pests and diseases that damage fruit and vegetables. The contrast between dreaming of a ripe, flavoursome tomato and surveying plants riddled with blight is harsh and makes planning for good disease management significant.

One of the biggest problems with growing edible plants is that by following the same routine year-in, year-out, we create a comfortable, predictable situation for pests and diseases.

Selecting disease-free stock

Nowhere is the notion of breeding against disease more pertinent or practised than in fruit and vegetable growing. The sheer commercial significance of producing a disease-free plant (reduced spraying costs, minimised risk of rejection by supermarkets) means resistance to disease is often ranked alongside or even above flavour as the most desirable characteristic. As in almost all areas of gardening, commercial drive creates the best developments and most fruit and vegetable catalogues feature extensive information on disease resistance.

This is not something that everyone will agree on, but with fruit and vegetable growing I think romance should go out of the window. If you have lost your deep-flavoured heritage tomatoes three years in a row to blight, should you try them again or look at a modern disease-resistant variety? Hedge your bets at least and mix several varieties together. My preference is always to intervene as little as possible and, for that reason, I let the plant breeder do some of the disease-resistance work for me.

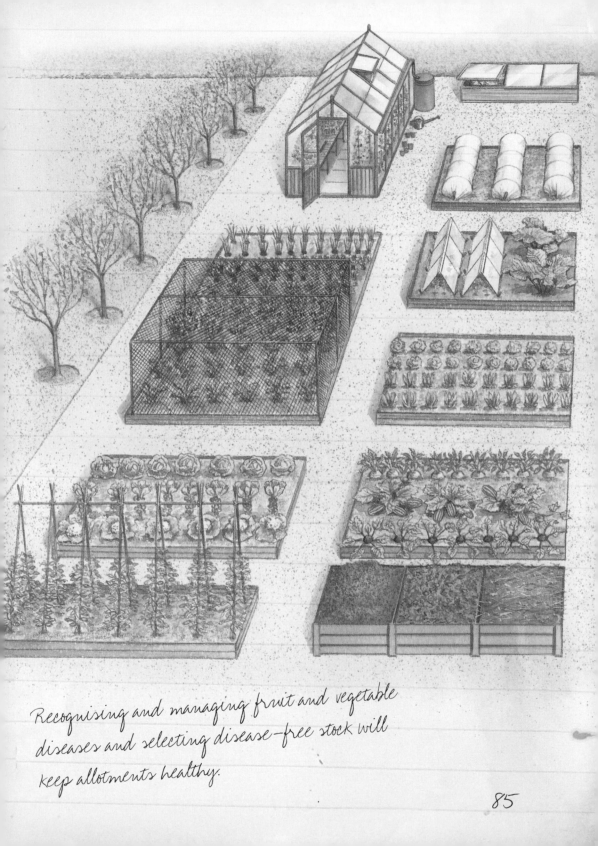

Recognising and managing fruit and vegetable
diseases and selecting disease-free stock will
keep allotments healthy.

Club root

This affects the brassicas (broccoli, cabbages, sprouts and cauliflower) and is potentially devastating. A fungal disease that breeds in the roots, it slowly shuts down the systems that move sugars and nutrients around the plant, leading to poor, stunted growth. As the fungus develops it distorts and eventually rots the root of the plant, ruining it completely.

Control

Club root is specific to brassicas and survives in the soil without them for up to five years. Crop rotation moves vulnerable crops away from the disease. Club root is less successful in alkaline soils, so the addition of lime can reduce its effectiveness, but this may not be sustainable in the long term. By sowing in the autumn, hardy brassicas can establish while club root is dormant and the disease is less likely to infect a strongly growing plant the following spring. Excellent club-root resistant cabbages ('Kilaxy') and cauliflowers ('Clapton') are available.

Choosing disease resistant cultivars is one of the best ways to avoid club root.

Tomato blight

Dark brown patches on the stem nodes and fruit are quickly followed by stunted growth and eventual death. Blight readily destroys whole crops and quickly establishes in the soil, with heavy rain splashing disease spores on to the plants.

Control

Blight thrives in wet summers, breeding quickly in humid conditions and using rain splash to move spores on to plants. Minimise the scope for the spores to enter by making any wounds as small as possible when you pinch out or defoliate (best done by snapping up rather than down). Mulching with disease-free organic matter or textile will also control spore movement. If the very early stages of blight are spotted, then a biological treatment such as *Bacillis subtilis* has the potential to reverse it. Apply every six to eight days until the plant is growing strongly. There are plenty of tomatoes available with blight resistance, such as 'Olivade'.

Potato blight

A close relative of tomato blight and a member of the infamous *Phytophthora* family, potato blight has deep historical and social significance for precipitating the Irish potato famine. A deadly disease, it first appears as yellow stunted growth that quickly turns black, with a white down forming on the underside of the leaf. The potato tubers rot, with dark browny-red spots on the skin.

Control

Potato blight is a serious disease, with no direct organic treatment. Removing potatoes from the bed after harvesting will stop the disease developing, as will rotation. Intensive vegetable production reduces the amount of beneficial microbes in the soil but use of green-waste composts and compost tea will make the soil more hostile to blight. Potatoes with blight resistance include 'Stirling', 'Cara' and 'Remarka'.

Cucumber and tomato mosaic virus

Viruses are a sinister bunch, not even classified as living by some scientific criteria. Often introduced to plants by feeding aphids, they inject their DNA into plant cells, reprogramming them to manufacture viruses. A very serious threat to food production, virus damage is recognised by the yellowish or pale green mottling on foliage, which can develop into brown streaks. Cucumbers and tomatoes grown under glass are most likely to be affected in a domestic garden, and the virus renders fruit unpalatably hard.

Control

Two big problems limit our ability to treat viruses: their inextricable link with the plant cells they have infected, and their extraordinary tolerance of temperature. There are no effective 'viricide' sprays and the ability of viruses to survive temperatures of 70°C means infected material cannot be composted. The only answer lies in prevention. Choose disease-free plants from a reputable source, manage aphid numbers to stop disease transmission and ensure your glasshouse plants are growing in fresh compost or soil you know you can trust.

Canker

Canker can be devastating to fruit trees. Caused by an air-borne fungus, canker initially enters the tree through wounds or pruning cuts and is recognised by distortions and swellings on the trunk that may weep. As the canker develops, the bark around the swelling will flake or break off while the disease weakens the tree to potentially fatal degree.

Control

Minimise the ways spores can enter the tree. Prune using the sharpest tools, ensuring cuts are clean and well executed. A ragged, excessive pruning wound offers a much bigger space for canker spores to infect.

Make sure when removing large branches that there is no danger of ripping bark off the tree. This can be done using the following method:

Pruning a large branch

This operation is done in several stages and it is vital that you use the right tool. A sharp pruning saw is ideal. Spend enough money and you can get high-grade Japanese steel that will be very sharp and flexible.

1 Start by undercutting the branch. Identify where the final cut will be and gently saw the underside of the branch, covering 50 per cent of the circumference. This stops the weight of the branch ripping the bark off the tree as it comes down.

2 Prune the branch back in several stages: this will gradually reduce the weight, making it easier to saw.

3 Saw off the final stub back to the branch 'collar'. This is a thickened ring of material in-between the branch and the trunk of the tree. Collars heal pruning wounds and should never be cut off. When pruned correctly the collar will close up, preventing the entry of canker spores.

Cutting a large branch in stages avoids damage to the tree, which can can encourage diseases such as canker.

Remove cankerous growth

Despite the destructive nature of the disease, canker can be fairly easy to contain. Often the disease is still contained in the first branch it infected. If left unchecked, this 'inoculum' will breed more spores and infect the rest of the tree, but if we remove whole, infected branches, we can remove the whole canker at point of entry.

Leaf curl

Often called peach leaf curl, it affects fruit trees in the rose family, such as plum, apricot and peach. It can look horrendous with young growth becoming discoloured, puckered and contorted.

It can be controlled by fungicides such as mancozeb, but the thoughtful gardener will think twice about this. Every season it looks like leaf curl will wreak havoc and yet, by the middle of the summer, the trees have recovered, new growth is healthy and fruit production is unaffected. Could we tolerate a bit of diseased growth? Should we replace the tree with something more suited to that spot? Or find a modern, disease-resistant variety?

weeds

I would never want to deny the pleasure of weeding to anyone, and it may come as no surprise to hear that there is no magic, professional method for eliminating weeds from our gardens. However, it is worth evaluating the best way to manage weeds thoughtfully, minimising energy use and not compromising the health of the garden.

Weedkiller

Should we use weedkiller in our gardens? Organic systems permit the use of concentrated vinegar (acetic acid), weed burners and mechanised hoes to control weeds but never glyphosate, a systemic weed killer (which circulates around the plant, killing it outright). Here lies one of the most contentious areas of gardening. Many argue that glyphosate is the most efficient and therefore most environmentally friendly way to

Perennial weeds, such as dandelions, are a challenge for the thoughtful gardener to eliminate.

control weeds. It may take multiple applications of vinegar or flames to eliminate serious weeds while glyphosate will do it in one, so which approach uses more energy or emits more carbon dioxide?

My approach is this. If you are organic, you have signed up to a system with set rules about what can and cannot be used and the glyphosate argument ends there. Effective alternatives are available and should be sought.

If you are not organic, glyphosate can have a role in your garden, but it is important to understand how this potent chemical should be used. Glyphosate should always be a means to an end, as it contains high levels of salt and excessive use will damage soil ecology. Plan a programme to eliminate the weed and then stop spraying. The most persistent perennial weeds are bindweed, dandelions, ground elder and thistle, and use of glyphosate should be restricted to these. Spray young, emerging leaves as they are more vulnerable and only apply when it is dry and not too hot, ensuring the chemical does not evaporate or get washed away. Follow the guidelines for mixing to the letter: it may be tempting to increase the strength, but this will just kill the leaves before the chemical has the chance to circulate and the plant will grow back.

Fallowing

Sometimes the only way to gain control is to stop gardening and start fallowing. If perennial weeds are starting to overwhelm a border, what is the most efficient way to eliminate them?

Bindweed in particular will worm its way deep into the roots of roses and herbaceous perennials, making it impossible to dig them out or spray. Fallowing is a big commitment, to write off part of your garden for one to two growing seasons, but the end result is deeply rewarding.

Fallowing a bed

To fallow is to leave an area in order to eliminate a specific weed, pest or disease. This decision is taken when all your horticultural efforts to reverse a developing weed problem are failing.

1 Fallowing starts in spring. Dig out any plants you want to keep, washing the roots in flowing water to clear away lingering bindweed. Divide herbaceous perennials very thoroughly, washing any crowns you want to retain. These plants should be put in a nursery bed and monitored for any sign of lingering weed infestation next year.

2 Any leftover plant material should be treated with caution. Put into the centre of a very hot compost heap or burn.

3 Spray to eliminate the weeds. With your garden plants gone, you can spray without causing damage and you should approach this as a one-off chance to eliminate problem weeds. Use a maximum of three applications and, by late September, no more weed shoots should be pushing through the soil.

4 Your bed will look miserable by the end of the growing season. The appearance of dead weed foliage and bare soil does not chime readily with the thoughtful gardener and you should return health to the soil as quickly as possible. Cultivate the soil lightly and sow a green manure of field beans, tares or grazing rye (see page 22).

5 The following spring, leave the green manure in until you are sure the perennial weed is completely eliminated. If so, cut down the foliage, add a large volume of organic matter and turn in using a fork or rotavator. Replace with clean plants.

93

Vinegar

Acetic acid weed killers are gaining in popularity due to increasing
restrictions on chemical use (especially in public areas) and it can be
effective, providing you understand its limitations. They scorch weed
foliage and burn through plant cells, which is enough to kill most annual
weeds. Vinegar will be less effective against mature perennial weeds that
sprout again from a strong root system. One of the best times for the
application of vinegar is in the spring when annual weeds can emerge
overnight in strong 'flushes'. Here, a swift application may be quicker
and more effective than hoeing.

Can I use vinegar from my cupboard?
Table vinegar will scorch weeds, but a proper formulated version
will do a better job.

Weed burners

These work on a similar principle to vinegar, burning weed foliage
to the point where it will not recover, either with direct flames or
by heating the plant using infra-red energy. Again, it is most effective
against annual weeds, but good-quality models (particularly infra-red)
burn broad-leaved weeds such as dock and dandelion so deeply that
they do not recover. Unless you have a large garden, you may consider
digging or hoeing the weeds more cost and energy efficient.

Mulching

Mulching can be used to help control weeds. By putting down a thick
layer of weed-free mulch in the spring, you inhibit growth of annual
weeds trying to germinate in the soil below. Perennial weeds are a
different matter and will simply grow through, so you should ensure
your soil is weed-free before applying a mulch.

However, mulching can contribute to ground elder elimination. Ground elder colonises new ground using thick white rhizomes that grow just under the surface. By placing very thick layers of mulch on top of problem patches, ground elder moves up to be near the surface. Carefully remove infested mulch and dispose of it by putting it in the centre of a very hot (70°C) compost heap or burn. Any ground elder that sprouts in the ground below will be weak.

Marigolds

One of the more attractive weed killers is *Tagetes minuta* (Mexican Marigold). Planted into a thick patch of ground elder or bindweed, a noxious chemical emitted from the marigold's roots will start to affect the growth of plants around it, and can eliminate weeds completely. A word of warning: to some, *Tagetes minuta* is a pernicious weed in itself and it can dominate. By stopping it from setting seed, a balance should be retained.

Mexican Marigolds emit chemicals that control weeds.

Pests

For virtually every plant that grows, there is a pest to threaten it. Are there any garden or glasshouse plants that do not have a couple of munches taken out of them? The thoughtful gardener accepts the presence of pests but grows plants that will never fully succumb to them, and finds clever tactics to reduce their impact to acceptable levels.

Most pests are defined by how they eat. Aphids, whitefly and leaf hoppers are 'suckers', injecting sharp-tipped feeding 'straws' (called stylets) into soft plant tissues to suck out sugar-rich sap. Slugs, snails, red spider mite and thrips are 'raspers', ripping off shards of plant tissue with sharp mouth parts and tongues.

Sucking insects damage plants in two ways: the physical impact of the stylet pushing into developing plants causes growth to distort. Even worse is the impact of poor dental hygiene: their stylets are covered in a variety of diseases, and as the aphid or whitefly hops from one plant to the next, it merrily transfers disease wherever it goes.

Understandably, plants are not that keen on having strips of plant tissue ripped off. A small infestation of thrip or red spider mite will disfigure the plant while a more serious attack could see all leaves being lost and potentially the death of the plant.

Controlling pests

There are two options when controlling pests: kill them at any cost (cheap, uncomplicated) or kill only the pest that troubles us (more expensive and less straightforward). What should define our decision is the ecological balance of the garden.

If we employ the bluntest insecticides to kill our particular pest problem, other insects will be killed too, be they pests or beneficial inhabitants of the garden, such as hoverflies, bees or ladybirds.

The best approach is the thoughtful, scientific one. What is the pest? When is it most vulnerable? Does it overwinter on our garden plants? Which natural, beneficial garden predators could help us control the pest and how do we ensure they are unharmed by our actions?

The best way to control pests in any garden situation is through integrated pest management. This means the use of beneficial predators and parasites in the summer, and controlled applications of an insecticide in the winter that will not harm desirable garden allies. Occasionally the balance tips and summer outbreaks occur – these are managed by a targeted summer spray.

Sticky soap and seaweed

Two of the best pest controls are also the least toxic. Insecticides derived from seaweed and soap will integrate neatly into a thoughtfully managed garden and will kill a wide variety of common pests.

They work through suffocation. Both horticultural soap and seaweed insecticide are viscous, sticky solutions that cling on to aphids and whitefly. This is a fatal development for the pests who breathe through a series of holes in their abdomens called spiracles. When coated in soap emulsion, the spiracles can no longer exchange oxygen and carbon dioxide, causing suffocation.

Why doesn't this harm beneficial insects?

It is important to visualise the ecosystem within a garden plant, such as a rose. Aphids are herbivores and, as their meals never run away, they have not developed the ability to move fast. Short, stumpy legs move the aphid from one feeding spot to the next at a gentle pace and when a wash of horticultural soap flows over the leaf, there is no chance of escape.

Predators such as ladybirds and hoverflies are quick and mobile, to enable the capture and killing of any potential meal. When a threat such as our insecticide approaches, they are simply agile enough to avoid it.

How to use 'gentle' insecticides

This type of insecticide will not give you the 'knockdown' (mass-murder) effect that more mainstream insecticides would. Anticipation of harmful insects is therefore vital:

— A weekly inspection of pest-prone plants in the garden and under glass will indicate whether biological control is working or pest levels are starting to build.

— Apply horticultural soap or seaweed insecticide immediately if the stem is covered in aphids or whitefly.

— Using a pressurised sprayer and a fine nozzle will make the job easier and allow consistent quantities of soap or seaweed to coat the pest infestation, ensuring a high success rate.

— Spray all over the plant, including the undersides of leaves. Spray until drips start forming and rolling off the leaves and stems. These products rely on direct, prolonged contact with the pest, so make sure they are coated.

— Always spray on a dry day when no rain is forecast; it is heartbreaking to watch two to three hours of hard work being washed away by a heavy shower!

— Apply 'pairs' of sprays, preferably linked to the lifecycle of the pest you are trying to eliminate. Gentle insecticides kill adult aphids and whitefly rather than any of the juvenile stages in their complex lifecycle. This means the pest adults we kill one day could be replaced by numbers of junior offspring several days later. Spraying six to eight days after the first application puts paid to this enterprising aphid behaviour.

Another way: physical control

As with the management of diseases, it is important to do everything possible to create a hostile environment for resident pests. It should be made as difficult as possible for pests to take hold before resorting to chemical controls.

Physical barriers can be extraordinarily effective. Pests often have to travel to our plants before they can cause any damage, so what happens if there is something blocking the way?

Carrot root fly barrier

Carrot root fly is one of the most damaging pests in a domestic garden and has the potential to ruin a season's harvest. However, this pest has one serious flaw in its biology: it cannot fly very high. With their normal flight trajectory at carrot-top height only, a barrier surrounding their feeding ground will cause them serious problems.

Erecting a carrot root fly barrier

1 Push a series of canes or link stakes around your carrots, allowing plenty of room to weed and thin your crop once the barrier is erected. If possible, use long canes and try to push at least one-third into the ground, making them very stable.

2 Attach the barrier to the canes. There are lots of useful materials available to make effective barriers, such as Enviromesh (a finely woven netting), clear plastic or horticultural fleece. Tie Enviromesh on to canes using twine or coated wire. Attach fleece using strong duck tape.

Sciarid fly sticky traps

Sciarid fly is a serious glasshouse pest. Easily recognised by the clouds of fast-flying, small black insects that rise in a flurry around young glasshouse plants, they quickly shred foliage and some plants will not recover. Just like root fly, however, sciarid fly has a distinct flight pattern, always flying low and directly from the surface of one pot to another. By using sticky traps we can both disrupt this flight pattern and physically trap large volumes of this troublesome pest.

Trapping sciarid fly

1 Carefully cut yellow or blue sticky traps into 2 x 2cm (¾ x ¾in) squares.

2 Place them horizontally on to the rims of your pots, wherever there is scope for sciarid fly to cross from pot to pot.

3 Replace the sticky squares when more than half the trap is covered in black sciarid flies.

Rabbit and deer fencing

The devastation caused by deer and rabbits is unmatched. A roe deer that happens upon your garden can remove all flowers overnight and leave you with trampled vegetation and hoof-prints as souvenirs.

Rabbits will mow down an extraordinary range of garden vegetation in a depressingly short space of time and, when the weather is cold, wreak havoc on trees and shrubs. Their love of soft, sweet 'sap wood' motivates determined damage to tree trunks and roots, with strong rabbit teeth perfectly capable of stripping thick bark away.

How to keep deer and rabbits out is one of the most frequently asked questions by desperate gardeners and the answer is simple: a fence. There are a host of products and remedies available claiming to repel rabbits and deer, ranging from bitter sprays applied to vulnerable foliage to lion dung. There is some limited evidence of their effectiveness, providing such products are applied on a regular basis and topped up after rainfall.

However, the thoughtful gardener will always seek out the most efficient solution and so we turn our attentions to fencing. Height and depth are required to keep rabbit and deer out. Digging in strong mesh to a depth of 60–75cm (2–3ft) will stop rabbits digging into your garden. This is best done at an angle and is very hard work, so I recommend employing a good fencing contractor.

Rabbit-proof fencing provides a barrier between your plants and garden pests.

To repel the most enthusiastic deer, a height of 1.5–2m (5–6½ft) is required, and it is vital the fence is strained tight along its length.

With rabbits and deer absent from your garden, life changes dramatically, with your energies available for gardening, rather than damage limitation.

Sticky pot rims for vine weevil

While vine weevil larvae are the biggest threat to our young plants, we should not take our thoughtful eye off the adults. Their curiously neat, geometric bites disfigure evergreen shrubs (such as rhododendron) and female vine weevils lay the eggs that become a whole generation of trouble for our young plants.

Vine weevil are closely related to beetles but, unlike them, they cannot fly. This allows the thoughtful gardener to undermine adult vine weevil mobility. Vine weevil adults like to lay their eggs into compost where their larvae can safely hatch out and gorge themselves on young plant roots. By adding a rim of sticky material such as barrier glue around the rims of pots, a physical barrier is in place that vine weevil adults cannot cross.

Glue bands

Using another technique to catch pests of limited mobility, glue bands are wrapped around the trunks of fruit trees at the end of the summer. The bands will trap or repel moths crawling up the tree to lay eggs during the autumn.

Bird netting can protect vulnerable plants from birds.

Bird netting

The only effective way to keep birds away from our fruit and vegetables, bird netting needs to be pegged down to keep the most determined blackbirds away. The speed at which birds can strip a crop means that netting should be constructed well in advance of fruit ripening.

beneficial predators and parasites

If your plants have been mangled by aphids or whitefly, it is reassuring to know that most garden pests have an enemy waiting to prey on them. It may be even more reassuring to know that these enemies are produced commercially, put in tubes and bottles and sold via mail order.

All major garden pests have a clearly identified parasite or predator, which controls their numbers. Of great interest to the thoughtful domestic gardener is the growing availability of biological controls on the 'amateur' market with many catalogues stocking a full range.

Although the majority of biological controls have been developed for glasshouse pests and glasshouse environments, several species are happy outside and will work well over the summer, controlling aphids on roses for example.

Biological control in the garden

— You must have pests for biological control to work. Perverse as it may be seem, it is more desirable to have low pest numbers than to eliminate your pest altogether. Most biological controls are very fussy about what they eat and if their chosen snack is not available when first introduced, they can quickly die.

The right habitat will encourage beneficial insects to stay in your garden.

— Pest levels should be low when the biological control is introduced. It is hard for them to munch their way through an aphid epidemic and it is unfair to expect biological control to achieve this. Give your new ally a good start by providing a manageable level of pests.

— Get conditions right. Biological controls often have fussy temperature, light and humidity requirements. Spending some time getting the conditions right or waiting for the right weather will give biological controls the best introduction to your garden.

— Provide a good habitat. Some biological controls establish in a garden or glasshouse after a handful of introductions and become an integral part of the ecosystem. Others need to be reintroduced every year, generally because of an inability to survive the winter. We can improve the chances of biological controls becoming resident by pandering to their house-making instincts. Lacewing houses are readily available, while some beneficial insects just want a nice shady spot for shelter.

Garden pests suitable for biological control

The following creatures can be discouraged with a variety of biological controls:

Whitefly

Whitefly can be controlled by a tiny parasitic wasp called *Encarsia formosa*. The wasp lays eggs in the whitefly's abdomen and, when the larvae hatch, the whitefly bursts in rather a brutal fashion. *Encarsia* are active from late March to October and are used in glasshouses, arriving on little white cards, which are secured near vulnerable crops. Introduce every two to three weeks and keep away from direct sunlight, preferably facing north or east.

Whitefly can also be controlled by a fungal disease called *Verticillium lecanii*, which is specific to whitefly. *Verticillium* is mixed with water and sprayed onto adult whitefly. The fungus breeds within the whitefly's body, forming long thin threads that weave their way through the abdomen and thorax. Eventually, the fungus becomes the dominant presence: the whitefly's internal organs are consumed, killing it and leaving the outer husk of the insect intact.

Mealybug

Mealybugs can be ontrolled by a beetle called *Cryptolaemus*. It is a voracious creature whose mobility allows rapid predation of their slow-moving prey. Happiest in the same warm, humid conditions as mealybug, *Cryptolaemus* needs patience to introduce, the woolly larvae crawling rather reluctantly out of their tubes, but can overwinter successfully.

Aphid

Aphidius is an aphid parasite that lays eggs into immature aphids. As the eggs hatch, the aphid ruptures. *Aphidius* females are very productive, laying up to 100 eggs in her lifetime. *Aphidius* arrives from the supplier as an adult, in tubes. To release, hang the tubes near infested plants, preferably with daytime temperatures of 18°C.

Slugs

The diverse world of nematodes – in particular *Phasmarhabditis hermaphrodita* – provides one of the more successful slug controls. Sold as Nemaslug, they arrive in a clay paste that is watered down (warm water mixes best) into solution and then applied to the soil around prone plants. The nematodes introduce a bacteria to the slug, which eventually kills our slimy foe.

Thrip

A large, aggressive predatory mite, *Amblyseius cucumeris* is not particularly fussy about what it eats, but luckily has a soft spot for the troublesome thrip. Generally it is sent out as larvae; *Amblyseius* pouches hung up near affected plants soon hatch out.

Red spider mite

Red spider mite can be controlled by an aggressive, predatory mite called *Phytoseiulus persimilis* that looks like a larger, angrier version of its prey. As soon as it is active it needs to eat red spider mites and should only be introduced once its preferred snack is active. This is an example of recognising early signs of a pest, in this case the little red or yellow streaks, on the topside of the leaf. At this stage *Phytoseiulus* can control red spider mite and save your plants. Leave it too long and it cannot.

Caterpillars

Steinernema carpocapsae is a nematode that needs to be applied regularly to combat the repeated hatchings that caterpillars are capable of. It should be used on prone crops, such as cabbages, from mid-July onwards.

Vine weevil

Steinernema krausei is another useful nematode worm that performs a heroic service: parasitising vine weevil larvae. Timing is everything. As this control is specific to vine weevil larvae, it needs to be applied in late summer as they are emerging.

General pests

Possibly the most voracious biological control of all, *Macrolophus* occasionally exorcises its hunger pangs on its human hosts (it bites). A willing predator of many glasshouse pests, including the destructive leafhopper, *Macrolophus* overwinters with shelter and should not need constant reintroduction. The main problem with *Macrolophus* is its voracious metabolism; if it cannot eat enough food when it is first released it can quickly die out.

The lacewing *(Chrysoperla carnea)* is also a 'generalist' predator, happy to munch on a wide variety of garden pests. It differs from *Macrolophus* because lacewings are easily established outside (they are a British native) and just as at home maintaining pest levels in a rose garden as they are in a glasshouse. Lacewings are generally bought in as larvae with the hatching adult doing the majority of the control. Some winter protection will encourage them to 'naturalise' in your garden and this is where installing lacewing houses will help them to survive.

Lacewings control a wide variety of pests.

disorders

When plants are deprived of the right nutrients, they quickly display symptoms of ill health, referred to as disorders. We need to assess whether the disorder can be reversed using a fertiliser, or whether it is the symptom of a deeper problem.

Nutrients for healthy growth

Nitrogen, potassium and phosphorus are referred to as major nutrients and when we buy fertiliser, the respective ratios of each is quoted. However, plants are equally dependent on an extraordinary array of micro-nutrients such as iron, manganese and molybdenum for complete health, sometimes only needing a microscopic fraction of one element.

Where do plants get nutrients from?

Plants get their nutrients from the soil — or, at least, a healthy, balanced soil. Technically, all the necessary nutrients should be available for the right plant growing in the right place in the wild. In this situation, a plant is completely self-sufficient.

Move to a garden situation and things can be very different. Poorly chosen plants, growing on badly maintained soil with no biology, may be so devoid of the right nutrients that they can only survive with added fertiliser. Does this sound like a healthy approach? If we were more thoughtful, could we move our plants closer to self-sufficiency?

Deficiencies

Put simply, a deficiency is a plant lacking a specific nutrient. Plants are wonderfully transparent about their feelings; if something is not right, it quickly manifests itself as discoloured foliage, aborted flowers or contorted stems. Although the absence of any of major- or micro-nutrient is an issue, there are five most common and debilitating deficiencies. Here is how to recognise them:

These five leaves show symptoms of the major deficiencies.

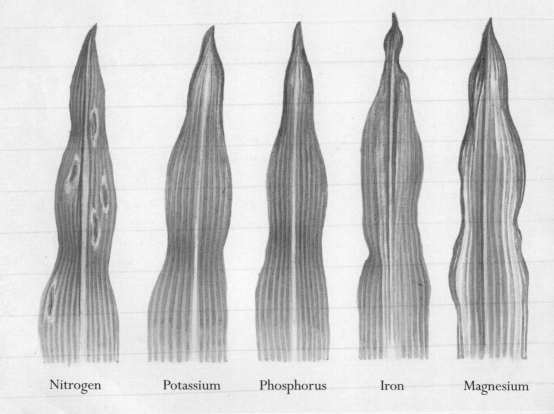

Nitrogen   Potassium   Phosphorus   Iron   Magnesium

The major nutrients

Nitrogen (N): produces green growth. Plants will use plenty of it when forming new leaves and stems. The quickest but perhaps not cleverest way to make a lawn grow quickly is to put a high volume of 'straight' nitrogen on it (see page 177 for alternatives).

Potassium (K): plays two main roles. It helps a plant produce healthy flowers and fruits, but also 'hardens' new, nitrogen-rich growth, making it tough and pest-resistant.

Phosphorus (P): plays a general role in overall growth and efficient photosynthesis. It also has a specific purpose in encouraging development of plant roots.

Nitrogen, potassium and phosphorus are highly interdependent in the way they affect growth. Too much nitrogen in the absence of potassium will cause lush, green growth that is too soft and floppy, making the plant prone to attack from fungal diseases. If there is too much potassium or phosphorus and not enough nitrogen when the plant is trying to grow actively, the leaves and shoots may be underdeveloped.

Iron (Fe) and magnesium (Mg) play similar roles. They both help a plant make chlorophyll, the pigment that not only makes plants green but also helps them turn the sun's energy into sugars, a process known as photosynthesis. An absence of either immediately affects the colour of the plant's leaves and their photosynthetic ability.

Plants are able to move magnesium from older leaves to the new leaves and buds, which are vulnerable and in need of the most nutrition. Iron is harder to move, which is why iron-deficient plants can have perfect green foliage everywhere apart from the newest leaves.

major nutrient deficiencies

DEFICIENCY	COLOUR OF LEAVES	TYPE OF GROWTH
Nitrogen	Orange, red or purple. Never green	Weak and distorted
Phosphorus	Brown spots on leaves	Can be distorted
Potassium	Brown, red or yellow scorching around edge of leaves	Soft and floppy. Poor, inconsistent flowers or fruits
Magnesium	Newest leaves and buds are green but old growth is yellow in-between veins	Withered leaves
Iron	Newest leaves and buds are yellow with green veins, old growth remains green	Foliage curls in

Fertiliser

The quickest way to remedy a deficiency is to add fertiliser. But the thoughtful gardener needs to ask why the plant became deficient in the first place. If we add fertiliser, will it be a one-off? Or will we be adding it regularly just to keep the plant healthy? We need to find out why the plant became deficient before deciding on a course of action.

What might cause a deficiency?

Waterlogged soil: could be full of nutrients with none available for plants to use. Plant roots could be surrounded by water, with the vital nutrient 'ions' simply too dilute to be useful. Nutrients such as iron, which aren't very soluble anyway, become useless to plants in very wet conditions.

Chalk soil: trees and shrubs need iron to be green, healthy and photosynthesising freely. Chalk soils readily lock useful iron into a 'useless' form that plants cannot absorb. Some plants are particularly sensitive to a lack of iron, with camellias being the worst offenders, and the sight of a yellowy, sick-looking camellia struggling on a chalk soil is not an inspiring one.

Fresh wood chip: fresh wood chip may seem a cheap and useful mulch, but its impact on the soil is not desirable. Fresh wood chip contains freshly exposed carbon, a substance that loves to team up with nitrogen. As the wood chip breaks down and enters the soil, nitrogen disappears and is no longer available for plants. This can quickly lead to yellow foliage as well as underwhelming growth.

If we think these events are one-offs, then adding the right fertiliser to get a plant growing healthily again is the correct approach. You will know in your heart how much you want to grow camellias on your chalk soil, but it might be worth choosing a plant that will be happier.

Choosing fertiliser to address deficiencies

A bewildering choice of fertilisers is available and it is important to look beyond colourful packaging and bold claims to work out what is in the bag. Nitrogen, phosphate and potassium (sometimes referred to as NPK) are normally listed in their ratio to each other.

Potassium (K) promotes good flower and fruit production on apple trees.

Understanding fertiliser ratios

NPK 2:1:4. Twice the volume of potassium (K) to nitrogen (N). This fertiliser is suitable for plants grown for their flower and fruit. For crops, the addition of a high-potassium fertiliser encourages good fruit production in strawberries, tomatoes and apples. If you are growing bedding plants, adding a high-potassium fertiliser encourages more flower buds to develop.

NPK 1:1:1. This is referred to as 'balanced' fertiliser and is best used early in the season to promote good overall growth in crops. A high-potassium fertiliser can be introduced later in the season to encourage flowering or fruiting. Balanced fertilisers can be used for pot-grown plants that are slow to grow and correct early signs of deficiency.

NPK 3:1:1. High-nitrogen fertilisers are rarely applied to ornamental or crop plants unless they are displaying serious deficiency symptoms, such as pale, stunted growth. This fertiliser gets lawns growing strongly in late spring and often includes iron to give grass a rich green colour. As explained earlier, high levels of nitrogen alone encourages soft, floppy growth that is disease prone and some potassium is required to 'harden' it.

NPK 1:3:1. Phosphate fertilisers are also used for lawns. When turf is first laid or grass seed sown, the application of 'super' phosphate or triple 'super' phosphate will encourage strong roots to develop, the foundation of a good lawn.

Organic or inorganic?

Both organic and inorganic fertilisers will achieve the results described opposite. What matters more is the balance of the garden.

Inorganic (synthetic) fertilisers are produced using chemical processes that have little in common with the soil. Repeated use of chemical fertilisers will change the balance of the soil. Changing salt and pH levels will be detrimental and numbers of beneficial bacteria, fungi and nematodes will start to drop, signalling a long-term decline in the health of the soil.

Another consideration is the carbon footprint of inorganic fertilisers. Their manufacture produces large volumes of carbon dioxide and global production of synthetic fertiliser is seen as a major driver of climate change. This is not to say that organic fertilisers do not have a carbon footprint, but it is significantly smaller.

Inorganic fertilisers work and deliver good, useful results for our plants. The question is whether they fit in with our long-term goals and can function as part of an ecologically balanced garden. My recommendation is therefore that organic fertilisers are used.

Types of organic fertiliser and tonics

Bonemeal: rich in phosphate, this could be used on an establishing lawn to encourage strong root growth. Added to soil when planting, bonemeal will encourage new trees and shrubs to root.

Chicken manure: fresh chicken manure is not suitable to be used directly on plants due to its high ammonia levels, which will quickly kill or seriously damage plants and unbalance natural elements in the soil. To make it usable, manure can be composted with some

Chicken manure makes an excellent fertiliser but needs to be composted with straw, sawdust or woodchip before use.

straw, sawdust or wood chip. An easier option is the purchase of pelleted chicken manure, which is heat-treated and processed into an easy-to-handle form. It is fairly nutritious stuff, almost balanced, but with slightly more nitrogen than potassium. The high volume of organic matter in chicken manure makes it a good soil improver that also works well on lawns.

Fish, blood and bone: a balanced (NPK 1:1:1) fertiliser. As with most organic fertilisers, it is relatively slow release and is suitable for a wide range of applications. You should avoid getting it on foliage, especially on a hot day, as it can scorch.

Hoof and horn: nitrogen-rich and slow-acting. Hoof and horn can be used as a base dressing around leafy vegetable crops and is also suitable for lawns.

Seaweed: although low on the major nutrients, seaweed is full of humic acid and trace elements and encourages strong, healthy growth. Seaweed is available in many forms, both liquid and granular, and seems particularly effective when used as a foliar feed (applying liquid fertiliser directly to the plant leaves). Some formulations of seaweed have extra nutrients such as iron.

Comfrey feed: although the plant is a bit of a weed, comfrey redeems itself by being of great benefit to the rest of your garden. Comfrey is normally steeped and made into solution (this is the perfect use for a council compost bin!). This is diluted at a rate of one part comfrey to 15 parts water and applied either to the foliage or roots of most garden plants. It is surprisingly nutritious and the high potassium levels make it useful for fruit-bearing crops such as tomatoes and strawberries.

Nettles: can be steeped in water in the same way as comfrey. The resulting liquid should be diluted by one part nettle to 10 parts water. Its high potassium content makes it a good tomato feed.

Mycorrhizal fertilisers: organic pellets inoculated with beneficial fungi. It is a highly effective product for maintaining health in trees and shrubs (although not ericaceous ones) and particularly good with roses. Mycorrhizal fertilisers should be applied two to three times during the growing season to maintain fungi levels.

Potash: any wood ash can be used as a fertiliser, providing you ensure the wood is clean and contains no chemicals – avoid MDF, for example. Bracken ash makes exceptional fertiliser for flowers and fruit, given its high potassium content.

Choosing plants

The garden is a series of habitats, some welcoming to plants, others more hostile. It is the staggering diversity of plants, our 'garden flora', accessible to gardeners that means the right plant is always available for the right place, and it is down to the thoughtful gardener to choose it.

some thoughts on choosing plants

Do you know where your nearest nursery (not garden centre) is? I only ask because this is the best place to buy your plants. The appeal of nurseries to the thoughtful gardener is their plant expertise and knowledge of what grows well in your area.

The first thing anyone should do when planning a new garden or redeveloping an existing one is to visit their local nursery to see what grows well. There may not be the bird seed or cups of freshly ground coffee you might find in a garden centre, but you will be able to speak to someone who has found the best group of plants for your area, and can show you how to grow them together.

Even if you are a bit nervous at first, you may find a meaningful conversation about plants and growing at a nursery one of the most rewarding experiences you will have as a gardener.

Questions to ask at your local nursery

How hardy is the plant? This is a complex issue but not a
topic that should be shied away from. Does the plant need winter
protection? Do you grow it in an exposed or sheltered spot?

Is it easy to grow? Some plants are stuck in the ground without
much ceremony and grow rapidly without any further intervention.
Others need their every whim attended to: only cut back in late
spring; feed with potash to get decent flowers; cover with a cloche
in the winter to stop it getting too wet, and so on. If you do not want
a hands-on challenge, it is worth checking whether your chosen plant
is self-sufficient in your area.

How docs it grow? How a plant looks in a pot is one thing, how it
will look after growing in your garden for three years is another. How
tall? How wide? Does it respond well to annual pruning? Will it set
seed everywhere or spread uncontrollably?

Some plants need more nurturing
than others, such as a cloche in
winter, for example.

What are your plants grown in? The issue of peat is one the most contentious in the horticultural world. It is true that gardeners, in the great scheme of things, do not use much of the peat that is extracted annually (a lot of it goes for power generation). It may be true that some aspects of peat harvesting, as the manufacturers claim, is sustainable. But to me, three irrefutable facts stand out.

— Peat bogs are one of the most important habitats in Northern Europe and have enormous wildlife value in the UK. Harvesting them, even if there is limited evidence of regeneration, affects the wildlife trying to live there.

— Peat bogs are immensely effective at 'locking up' carbon. If we are trying to reduce the amount of carbon in the atmosphere, then why are we undermining one of nature's most effective ways of redressing the balance?

— There are some decent, if not perfect, alternatives to peat available to all nurseries.

There are endless debates about peat alternatives and, to be fair to nurseries, some plants are very hard to grow in non-peat composts, particularly ericaceous subjects such as magnolias. However, herbaceous plants will grow very happily in composts made from pulverised wood or green waste. Even if you end up having nothing more than a 'great peat debate', it is still worth asking at your nursery. Some of our best herbaceous plant nurseries now grow peat-free and the National Trust only uses peat-free compost (see pages 155–156 for more information about alternatives to peat).

right plant, right place

In the rest of this chapter we are going to look at a variety of different garden habitats, and explore groups of plants that will flourish in them. A garden where no plant will grow is a rare thing: the thoughtful gardener will employ the tried-and-tested principle of 'right plant, right place' to ensure the best choice is made.

What's in a name?

I will not regale you here with a wealth of Latin names, but I would like to share some basic elements of plant naming (nomenclature) with you.

— **Genus:** a botanical rank that groups together a number of species. The genus is given in Latin at the beginning of plant names, for example *Papaver* orientale 'Patty's Plum'.

— **Species:** a group of closely related individuals able to breed with each other. The species is also given in Latin following the genus, for example *Papaver* **orientale** 'Patty's Plum'.

— **Variety:** a naturally occurring variation on a species, which is usually indicated at the end of the plant name, for example *Sarcococca hookeriana* **var. *digyna***.

— **Cultivar:** a variation on a species created through breeding: either a cross between two plants or an 'accidental' seedling with new characteristics. The cultivar is given at the end of plant names in English, for example *Papaver orientale* **'Patty's Plum'**.

— **Annual:** a plant that lives, flowers, sets seed and dies in one growing season.

— **Biennial:** a plant that grows one season and flowers, sets seed and dies the next. Some biennials sometimes grow as triennials, with two seasons of growing and one of flowering, seeding and dying.

— **Perennial:** a plant that lives for three years or more and, in the broadest sense, this word can encompass everything from a geranium to an oak tree. Perennials that live for the minimum period are called, predictably, 'short-lived'.

plants for dry places

The perfect dry garden is one that requires virtually no input from the thoughtful gardener. All the plants growing in it will be adapted to poor soil so there will be no need to dig in compost to retain moisture or, for that matter, gravel to improve drainage. Our poor-soil plants will have no need for fertiliser, so none should be added. The plants chosen survive whole summers without rainfall, so there will be no need for irrigation and this lack of water should also deter a lot of weeds.

The majority of plants that thrive in dry places are from the Mediterranean climate zones of the world. That includes California and Mexico, the Western Cape of South Africa, Western Australia and Northern Chile as well as the Mediterranean basin. The Mediterranean climate is defined exactly as a six-month dry summer followed by a mild, wet winter with only short periods of frost. The wonderful array of plants adapted to grow in these conditions is simply staggering.

The best-known group from this climate are the silver leaf plants:
lavenders, rosemary, *Stachys* and *Cistus* have pungent foliage and are
covered in fine hair that prevents water evaporation in intense heat.

Lavenders

Of this group, perhaps only lavender works well planted *en masse*
(lavender hedges can be very effective if planted densely) with cultivars
such as 'Munstead' and 'Hidcote' responding well to a late summer cut
that removes all annual growth but does not cut into hard wood.

Lavender (Lavandula angustifolia) is perfect for dry gardens.

Many new cultivars arrive every year, such is the commercial value of lavender, with many being based around the French *Lavandula stoechas* group, such as 'Regal Splendour', 'Kew Red' and 'Tiara'. The plants are compact, the flower heads large and the colours tend to be striking and intense. A word of warning when choosing them: they have very little hardiness and can be lost in extended temperatures of -5°C. They may be best grown in the mildest part of the garden, or made part of an annual propagation regime.

Lavender aside, other 'typical', woody Mediterranean plants struggle to bring garden value when planted alone. The tendency to become 'leggy' (tall and gaunt) on rich temperate soils devalues their garden role and this is particularly true of *Cistus*, which never looks better than when it is growing on a rocky Greek hillside.

You need to apply a broader approach to Mediterranean climate planting. The eryngiums, a wide variety of fine, architectural grasses, the bulbs and tree heaths of South Africa and the annual meadow flowers of California, are all perfectly adapted to relentlessly dry garden areas but will bring all the diversity of form, colour and growth habits needed to garden and design creatively.

Eryngiums

A particularly rewarding group of herbaceous plants, eryngiums create a feeling of arid exoticism with ease. Amazingly enough, in the wild, eryngiums span two continents and the Atlantic Ocean, growing in both mountainous regions of Europe and South America. Also known as the sea hollies, they are instantly recognisable with barbed, strap-like leaves and dense, prickly flowers.

Eryngium giganteum 'Miss Willmott's Ghost' is a striking plant suited to dry environments.

Most striking of the European representatives are variations on *Eryngium bourgatii*, including the electric colouring of 'Picos Blue' and the newer 'Picos Amethyst'. The tale of *Eryngium giganteum* 'Miss Willmott's Ghost' is embedded in garden folklore. The wealthy, brilliant and eccentric Victorian gardener Ellen Willmott is said to have distributed seed of *E. giganteum* without invitation in any garden she visited. Whether this 'gift' was welcomed or not is another matter.

I enjoy the early part of *E. giganteum's* life: strong, flat, exquisitely patterned rosettes grow without flowering one year, but by the time the enormous flower spike emerges in the second year, the plant starts to look rather coarse.

The South American eryngiums tend be larger and more exotic looking. *Eryngium agavifolium* is spectacular but, quite frankly, savage with great hooks covering the edges of its large glossy leaves. Plant sparingly, as it tends to fill favourable conditions quickly. Slightly more elegant is *Eryngium eburneum,* which has slimmer leaves and a more delicate flower spike.

South African shrubs and perennials

There is a bit of a myth surrounding the hardiness of South African shrubs that photos of a snow-clad Table Mountain should dispel. The wet and cold British winter threatens South African plants far more than simple sub-zero temperatures, and we should choose only the most free-draining soil for them.

The size, colour and complexity of *Protea* and *Leucadendron* flowers never cease to amaze and their status as 'garden aristocrats' is rightly held. Of similar appeal are their silvery, felted foliage and a versatile, rounded habit. They are difficult, but not impossible to grow, and warm, sunny sheltered gardens should explore the possibilities. *Proteas* and *Leucadendrons* are unusually sensitive to phosphorus levels in the soil and I recommend you test for this nutrient first. NPK testing kits are available by mail order or online and the test is quick and easy.

I would try growing *Leucadendron argenteum,* which is silvery leaved and hardy to -6°C with yellow, tulip-shaped flowers, and *Protea cynaroides* (the king protea), which bears the definitive, giant, pink-crimson protea flowers if protected from frost.

Tree heathers such as *Erica canaliculata* (white flowered) and *Erica discolor* can become fairly stately in sheltered spots, achieving heights well over 2m (6½ft) without losing their shape. *Eucomis* (the pineapple lily) are perfectly hardy in sandy soil and pleasingly vigorous, although the bronze-leaved forms do not combine that well with other foliage.

There are many other South African bulbs that can grow outside in skilled hands and there are several specialist bulb nurseries that can satisfy further interests. Associations with the blousy florists' gladioli should not detract from the beauty of species *Gladiolus,* which occupy a different realm of subtlety. *Gladiolus papilio* is tall and slender with cream flowers, tinged with green and a little pink. *Agapanthus* get rather dense and lose flowering vigour on rich earth, but providing they are divided regularly and grown in thin sandy soil, there can be little to match the late summer displays of *Agapanthus inapertus* 'Lydenberg' and *Agapanthus* 'Purple Cloud'.

Mediterranean climate grasses

There is a distinct quality that marks out Mediterranean grasses: fine, slender foliage, striking flowers and a special ability to reflect light make them fine garden plants. Adding to their appeal is the minimal amount of maintenance they require: the occasional comb through to remove old foliage; a shear down in mid to late spring to stimulate new leaves; and lifting and dividing (see page 162) every five to seven years to stop the clump getting too dense.

Helictotrichon sempervirens (blue oat grass) forms a striking hummock with slender blue-grey foliage and wispy, oat-like flowers. Give it plenty of space — it can form a 1.4m (4½ft) wide clump — and allow it to be a focal point in a mixed border or informal planting.

Hordeum jubatum (squirrel tail grass) is utterly charming. Small and discrete, the slender foliage shimmies in the slightest summer breeze and it will happily occupy space at the front of a border or near a path. Its exotic feathery flowers are cream, tinged with pink, and pale green seed heads follow. *Hordeum jubatum* is an annual, best perpetuated by collecting and sowing seed. It may self-sow in favourable conditions.

With a careful choice of plants, a Mediterranean planting can be achieved in British gardens.

Briza maxima (greater quaking grass) is another compact grass that moves seductively in the wind. It has remarkable, densely plaited flowers, topped with iridescent purple caps reminiscent of an exotic, tropical insect. Adding to the sensual experience is the dry rustle of the seed heads when the breeze blows and it is a shame to cut them down.

Plant low drifts of *Eschscholzia californica* and *E. lobbii*, *Tolpis barbata*, *Clarkia repens* and *Argemone mexicana*; wisps of *Hordeum jubatum*; punctuation points of *Yucca whipplei*, *Yucca gloriosa* and *Eryngium agavifolium* and *Eryngium* 'Picos Blue', and colourful spikes of *Watsonia*, *Tulbaghia* and *Gladiolus*. *Erica canaliculata*, *Cercis siliquastrum* and *Leucadendron* provide height and winter form.

plants for boggy places

Boggy parts of your garden should induce joy and excitement, rather than despair. This may sound glib if you have struggled with a waterlogged site, but if you visit the best bog gardens you will see lush foliage, vibrant colour and a huge palette of plants to work with.

Many bog plants come from the species-rich low altitude areas of the Himalayas. Here, a quick turnaround is required as the plants have to grow and flower during the period of late spring and early summer snow-melt. This may be a reason why they flower with such vibrancy and colour, with a limited and short-lived population of insects to attract to pollinate them.

Primulas

Primula flowers provide some of the brightest stars of the bog garden. Different primula species grow remarkably well together, with the candelabra and drumstick groups making spectacular spring displays. *Primula denticulata* will provide purples and occasionally whites (primulas are a very promiscuous group, readily cross-breeding and producing new variations), while *Primula vialii* is reminiscent of a firework with its cone flowers of deep purple and red. Soft oranges are provided by *Primula bulleyana*, a species that has inspired a wide variety of hybrids, and yellows come from *Primula florindae*. When these species (and others) are grown *en masse*, especially around a stream or pond, the result is never less than breathtaking.

Himalayan poppies

Growing Himalayan poppies should come with some words of caution. If successful, the results may be the most spectacular thing your garden has ever known, but this group of plants is extremely condition specific. If your garden doesn't have the right conditions, do not pursue them. If you have a cool climate, some shade, deep soil that remains damp in the summer and plenty of organic matter then there is every chance they will grow. They undoubtedly grow better in the north of the UK, with Scotland being their British stronghold; however, a shady bed, which faces east and therefore gets some sun, could be ideal.

Most famous of all is the blue poppy, *Meconopsis betonicifolia*. The depth and clarity of colour in the flowers is breathtaking and their short flowering period only seems to

The majestic blue poppy (Meconopsis betonicifolia) will thrive in a cooler environment.

add to their allure. In the wild, *M. betonicifolia* is found in rocky, mid-altitude areas of the Himalayas, but this is deceptive as they have a knack for seeking out deep seams of organic matter, normally leaf litter, and have surprisingly long roots to anchor into this nutritious stuff. In the garden this means one thing: leaf mould and plenty of it.

Meconopsis really benefit from being divided in the spring: if you look closely you'll see two to three plants in each clump, and careful dividing will mean a massive increase in your display. Take this opportunity to work a decent volume of leaf mould into the soil.

There are white forms available (*Meconopsis betonicifolia* var. *alba*) and *Meconopsis grandis* is also worth trying: a little bigger and earlier flowering. In some respects, *Meconopsis horridula* lives up to its name, being extensively covered in slender, mean-looking spines, but it is a truly beautiful plant, tall – around 80–90cm (30–35in) – and imposing, with a deep bluey-purple flower.

Other plants for damp places

Astilbe grow in tight, shapely clumps and have the terrific asset of attractive flowers and foliage. Feathery flower spikes, which tend to be white or pink, catch early sunlight very effectively, especially when they are covered in spring dew. *Astilbe* 'Fanal' has dark foliage and striking scarlet flowers and contrasts well with whites such as *Astilbe* 'Bridal Veil'.

Rodgersia are wonderful foliage plants, which are lush, exotic and easier to grow in the domestic garden than the likes of Gunnera. They have usefully descriptive names: Rodgersia sambucifolia (leaves like a green elder tree) has fine, divided foliage, while Rodgersia aesculifolia (foliage like a horse chestnut) has large, familiarly shaped five-fingered leaves.

Rheums, or ornamental rhubarbs, are another foliage plant that will grow merrily in damp spots, although also tolerant of relatively dry, shady ground. Some people find rhubarbs such as Rheum palmatum a little coarse, and there can be no doubting their desire to dominate. However, it is always about finding the right plant for the right place, and a large dell or boggy woodland area could look very dramatic planted with rhubarbs.

Erythronium, or dog-toothed violets, are absolute charmers, happy in humus-rich soil or damp meadow grass; they conduct themselves with discretion and dignity, producing nodding, pagoda-shaped flowers from neat, tightly formed rosettes. Erythronium dens-canis comes from Europe and emerges at the first hint of spring, bearing mauve flowers. E. revolutum comes from America and is a little larger with the wide variety of hybrids derived from this plant flowering from pink to white. It should happily naturalise in the same conditions as E. dens-canis, flowering a few weeks later.

plants for cold parts of the garden

In the UK, north and easterly winds create a permanently icy blast for six months of the year, frost takes an age to thaw and seemingly nothing grows. Many of us have parts of the garden that are downright cold and this is where extra thought is needed if some horticulture is to thrive.

Hardiness is mentioned earlier in this book (see page 119) and, in this instance, it is important to see it as a complex, multi-faceted concept. It is not just about mild gardens and cold gardens. Some plants can tolerate cold winds but will be killed by direct exposure to sub-zero temperatures; for others, the exact opposite applies. Some plants will be hardy in sandy, free-draining soil, but will quickly die in waterlogged conditions over the winter. Without fail, tracing a plant back to its wild origins will provide you with bountiful information about its suitability for your garden.

When looking for cold-tolerant plants, low-lying parts of Northern Europe, Asia and America will provide plenty of options. Alpine plants are generally very hardy but bring complications: they are intolerant of winters and wet or very hot summers, so it is easy to see why they are often grown in specialist glasshouses. Parts of Scotland can provide the right habitat.

Cornus (or the dogwoods)
The full name of the predominant garden dogwood, *Cornus alba* 'Sibirica', says it all: these are indomitably hardy plants, used to cold places and, luckily for us, are dramatic and showy into the bargain.

Although planted mostly for their displays of autumn and spring colour, *Cornus* hold their own in the summer, provided they are planted in the right numbers.

There was a time when dogwood would come in just the two colours, the red of *Cornus alba* 'Sibirica' or the yellow of *Cornus stolonifera* 'Flaviramea'. Not any more. If you have space, a full-spectrum wave of dogwood cultivars gives a stunning effect, and will look even more spectacular if they can be reflected in some still water.

Cornus alba 'Kesselringii' is a deep, velvety black that looks most striking when surrounded by a dusting of snow. The evocatively named *Cornus sanguinea* 'Midwinter Fire' is bred from our native dogwood and could not be more removed from 'Kesselringii', being a sharp, vivid orange, touched with red. If the traditional *Cornus alba* seems a little dull, why not try its richer, brighter (if rarer and more expensive) cultivar, 'Baton Rouge'. Also of great charm is a cultivar named after the great arboretum 'Westonbirt', which has a fine white, waxy down on the stems that seems to enhance the tone of red.

Very hardy foliage plants

Chamaerops humilis is a surprising palm, being one of the most sculptural and the most hardy. Redolent of Riviera roadside plantings, it is actually hardy down to -13°C. In a similar vein, some of the more exciting, architectural ferns are also super-tough. *Dryopteris erythrosora* (Japanese shield fern) has red-bronze tints to its finely etched fronds, while the wiry *Blechnum spicant* (hard fern) and lusher, trunk-forming *Blechnum magellanicum* are perfectly hardy.

Hydrangea aspera 'Villosa' will create a stunning display in cold areas of the garden.

Hydrangeas

Hydrangeas are a hardy lot, many growing in the icier parts of Eastern Asia, Chile and North America. Often overlooked is the climbing *Hydrangea seemannii*, an evergreen that willingly colonises chilly east-facing walls and charms everyone with its creamy 'lacecap' flowers. *Hydrangea quercifolia* will star in any garden: deeply cut leaves reminiscent of an oak, that turn bronze-purple in the autumn, tolerance of shade and cold, and a perfect neat habit that never straggles. *Hydrangea aspera* 'Villosa' (a confusingly named plant, but as long as you quote *aspera* and 'Villosa' you will get the right thing) is a noble plant. Standing well over 2m (6½ft) tall, its upright stems are covered with flaky, golden bark. The leaves are velvety and the flowers a rich bluey-purple.

plants for sheltered parts of the garden

The UK has much to thank the Gulf Stream for. Despite the northerly location of the British Isles, the warm Atlantic air that the Gulf Stream brings to the west has an extraordinary, moderating effect on UK winters. The west coast of Scotland is the most extreme example of the Gulf Stream's influence – despite a latitude in line with that of the Baltic states, gardens here can grow plants from South Africa and Australia without protection.

This climatic fluke is one of the key reasons why the variety of garden flora is so vast in the UK; no matter how far flung the plant's origins or how disparate its native climate, there always seems to be a corner of the British Isles that will provide a suitable environment in which the plant can flourish.

Of course, our gardens have great climatic variety within them. Many of us have a sheltered wall in our garden that feels positively warm on sunny winter days, or perhaps an exposed bed where easterly winds always seem to blow. If we know an area is sheltered, where perhaps the frost does not linger, then what is to stop us from experimenting?

Some of the most dramatic garden effects can be created with borderline hardy plants. Spectacular foliage plants from subtropical and Mediterranean climates can create a jungle effect that feels lush, luxuriant and undeniably exotic. While this style can be created using annual or seasonal planting, it is a little bit more exciting if it can live in the garden permanently without too much fuss.

Simple insulation can protect tender plants in winter.

The key to establishing a successful subtropical planting is to get the plants through two or three winters. By this point the plants, even if tender, will have had time to adapt to their environment and will crucially have developed some tough, potentially woody outer growth to offer some insulation.

My general rule with gardening is to leave plants to find their own way. If, however, we want to get experimental, this rule might have to go on hold briefly. However, this is a means to an end. By exploiting a mild part of the garden, we are still following the principles of the thoughtful gardener by choosing the right plant for the right place. By seeking out the most exciting and stimulating planting options we are also expressing the innate creativity within any good gardener. By employing a few tricks we can satisfy both instincts.

Although every instinct of mine is to plant in the autumn, subtropical planting is one area where I make an exception. A late spring planting will give the subtropical plant a whole growing season without frost, allowing it to become established and, crucially, form a strong root system capable of regenerating the plant should the worst happen.

Another intervention permitted in the name of pushing back boundaries is some winter protection. Not year after year of mollycoddling you understand, but just enough insulation to get the plant through the crucial first two or three winters. It pays to be flexible and get the plant used to cold (1–5°C) without protection, but check the weather regularly: frost is normally predicted with great accuracy and flagged up with enough time to act.

Assessing your microclimate

A useful acquisition for any thoughtful gardener is one or two minimum-temperature thermometer(s). By recording how cold the garden gets, and comparing different areas, you can assess whether your microclimates are perceived or real. Once you can confirm your sheltered bed really is 3–4°C warmer, you can start selecting less hardy, more exotic plants. Good plant books tell you what 'minimum night temperature' a plant can stand and, armed with your own garden data, you will know whether you can grow it.

protecting borderline plants

Fleece

'Horticultural' fleece is widely available from large garden centres or good mail-order firms and comes in different weights. It offers limited frost protection although, over time, cold, damp air can build up under the fleece, paradoxically threatening to chill the plant. For this reason, if fleece can be applied in response to a frost warning and then removed during periods of milder winter weather, plants can 'breathe' and fresh air can circulate. To make winter protection with fleece:

1 Create a square wooden frame from 2 x 2in (5 x 5cm) batten.

2 Staple the fleece on to the frame (with a double fold where the staple enters) with a staple gun. A couple of different sizes of fleeced frame to place over acclimatising semi-tender plants will be very useful.

3 Fleece can also be draped directly over a tender plant, although a really hard frost has the ability to chill the plant directly where it touches the fleece. Using some canes or bricks to lift it off the plant slightly will avoid this risk.

Bracken

A downright pest when it is threatening to swamp plants in the summer, bracken becomes a useful tool to the thoughtful gardener in the winter. Dead fronds can create sheaths of warm, dry, straw-like insulation with a multitude of uses. To use bracken for winter protection:

1 Arrange thick bundles of dry bracken fronds around *Gunnera* heads, banana stems and tree fern growing points.

2 Secure with some netting, twine or rhubarb or *Gunnera* leaves.

3 Layers of bracken fronds will provide wonderful insulation when laid on top of tender bulbs such as *Anigozanthus* (kangaroo paw), *Watsonia* or *Tulbaghia*.

Bubble wrap

Bubble wrap of the large bubbled, heavy-duty variety makes for an effective insulating material – less attractive than fleece but slightly warmer and harder wearing. Applied to simple frames, tunnels and cloches it can add several degrees of warmth over the winter, which is enough to stop a frost from being fatal. Heavy-duty bubble wrap also makes an effective extra layer of insulation on a glasshouse in the colder months of the year. Added in single- or double-layer sheets to the sides of a glasshouse, it will stop the rapid heat loss that can make winter heating so inefficient.

Pipe lagging

Pipe lagging is useful for woody plants with long, thin trunks. Without thick layers of woody protection, the water and sap columns within the plants can freeze and if this is prolonged, irreparable damage can be done to the plants' cells. Lagging comes in many dimensions – allowing several diameters of trunk to be covered. The convenient slit down the side makes wrapping around the trunk straightforward and a wrap of horticultural fleece over the top will complete an effective insulation.

plants for sheltered spots

Many of the 'subtropical' plants commend themselves to us with their lush, luxuriant foliage. Palms such as *Washingtonia filifera, Jubaea chilensis* (Chilean wine palm) and *Butia capitata* make an exciting change from hardy palms and can be grown readily in sheltered spots of UK gardens. Contrasting the spiky palm foliage with the broad, rounded shapes of *Canna* and banana (*Musa basjoo*, *M. velutina*) will be extremely effective.

Scheffleras

Scheffleras definitely belong under the heading 'plants that should be better known'. These exotic relatives of the ivy hail from the Far East, including Taiwan and Vietnam. The best-known member of this group is *Schefflera actinophylla* or the umbrella plant, which is widely grown as a house plant. Surprisingly, it has several relatives that will grow readily outside, unequivocally delivering the wow factor to your garden.

Scheffleras such as *S. alpina*, *S. taiwaniana* and *S. macrophylla* bring sculpted, architectural stems and large, lush leaves with vividly coloured stems to your border with virtually no fuss. Happy to combine with *Hedychiums*, bananas and small palms, they will prove fairly hardy, especially if they make it through their first winter and are kept away from cold winds.

A couple of spectacular shrubs

Two complementary shrubs that will elicit gasps of delight from your guests (and you) when they flower are *Clianthus puniceus* and *Erythrina crista-galli*. *Clianthus* (also known, tellingly, as the Lobster Claw) is a shrub in the pea family that never gets particularly large and has a fairly slender, weeping habit. It still comes as a surprise to me to see it flower.

142

gladioli species make a beautiful addition to sheltered borders.

In late April or early May, faintly ridiculous 'claws' of bright scarlet tumble down from the previously inconspicuous shrub in great abundance. If you find scarlet a bit overpowering, there is a cool white form (*C. puniceus* 'Albus'). It is definitely a touch on the tender side, and late frosts can be disastrous for flower buds.

Erythrina crista-galli, also in the pea family, rejoices in the exotic common name of Brazilian coral tree and is found in several South American countries. If well situated against a south or south-west facing wall, it will produce coral-red flowers in great, dense trusses, also reminiscent of claws in their shape. From a distance it appears that a swarm of extraordinary moths has descended.

Some tender bulbs

Ginger lilies (*Hedychium*) can become a bit too successful in sheltered beds, but providing they are split down every three or four years, there will always be more exotic flower spikes than overwhelming foliage. Many bulbs ask for nothing more than free-draining soil and an absence of persistent frost to survive the winter.

South African natives *Watsonia, Nerine bowdenii, Tulbaghia* and *Gladiolus* work well together, and bear flowers and foliage separately, increasing the wow factor at flowering time. Another group of bulbs that should be tried in sheltered spots are the *Narcissus tazetta* from the north-east Mediterranean, North Africa and the Canary Islands. *Tazettas* are light, slender and joyous to look at, bearing multi-headed flowers of white or sharp yellow.

143

Macaronesian plants

The Canary Islands and Madeira, which along with the Azores are collectively known as the Macaronesian Islands, only experience frost at their highest altitudes. Most plants growing there only know about wet and dry seasons and yet can succeed surprisingly well in UK gardens. The geographical isolation of the islands has produced a very distinctive group of plants, quite unlike those from nearby Europe and they look great planted together. The growing movement towards borderline hardy plants means that more Macaronesian species are available than ever, either as seed or plants, and now is the time to try them.

The extraordinary *Melanoselinum decipiens* is one of the best places to start. Fed to grazing cattle in the Canaries, this giant umbellifer can readily grow to 4.5m (15ft) and looks wonderfully exotic with its twisted, ribbed stem and deeply glossy foliage. It makes sense to find something else to match this size and there can be no better flowering plant to do this than *Echium pininana*. The giant spikes of purple-blue flowers have long been one of the great spectacles of the mild south-western gardens, but given free-draining soil and winter shelter from frost, this plant can be grown anywhere.

Think of *Euphorbias* and *E. mellifera* (syn. *E. longifolia*) may not come to mind. A large shrub, up to 3m (10ft) high and 3–3.6m (10–12ft) wide, its abundant lime-green flowers produce an intoxicating honey scent (*mellifera* means honey flowered) and are a great hit with the garden's insect population. On hot days in late summer, the seed heads burst open to distribute the seed as far as possible with a loud crack, reminiscent of popping corn.

plants for shade

The perception that planting for shade is a challenge is a false one. Shade-loving plants are some of the loveliest of all and give us the finest winter and early spring displays.

The challenge that shade-growing plants face in the wild is an immense one, as they must race to flower and get pollinated before the dense woodland canopy of summer develops. The limited number of insects active in the winter adds further intensity to the challenge and shade-dwelling plants have responded with some truly spectacular tactics to get noticed. Vividly coloured flowers and the sweetest fragrances bring inspiration and joy into our gardens, often as winter threatens to cast misery over our state of mind.

Daphnes

Daphnes deserve a place in any garden. Is there any winter-flowering shrub that smells as sweetly? For me, it is the winter fragrance champion, to the point where some people find it intoxicating, and a cut sprig of flowers can quickly overpower a small room. Daphnes grow readily in good soil in a sheltered position with a little organic matter and can tolerate (but not thrive on) chalk.

Daphne bholua is arguably the most garden-worthy of this group; plump waxy flowers sit proudly on bare wood, in great abundance and its scent merits it being sited near a path or bench. *Daphne bholua* 'Jacqueline Postill' is a strong, upright plant with rich pink flowers that surprises some with its eventual height and spread, so it needs plenty of space. *D. bholua* 'Darjeeling' is very tolerant of cold and has paler white flowers, touched with a hint of pink.

Witch hazels

Like Daphnes and *Chimonanthus*, the impact of witch hazel flowers is greatly increased by their appearance on bare stems, right in the heart of winter. The spidery flowers cling tightly to the branches and many emit a subtle, rather charming perfume.

Anyone seeking to create a shady winter garden with any impact should seek out this group of plants, particularly to reward the unstinting efforts of plant breeders such as Chris Lane and Robert and Jelena De Belder, who have endeavoured to bring a huge new palette of rich colours to us.

The variety of flowers available (more than 120) is a little bewildering, but given their eventual size – a spread of 2–3m (6½–10ft) – adding just two or three to your garden may be enough. *Hamamelis mollis* originates from China and has spawned a number of clear yellows, with the gold of 'Wisley Supreme' probably the pick of the bunch.

When *H. mollis* is crossed with its Japanese cousin, *H. japonica*, very exciting things happen. Referred to as the x *intermedia* group, rich reds and oranges are introduced. It is difficult to narrow down the x *intermedia* group to a few choices, but *H.* 'Barmstedt Gold' seems to glow in cool winter light. *H.* 'Aphrodite' is a sharp, vibrant but not tacky orange and the deep, rich reds of 'Diane' or the newer 'Twilight' may be the perfect choice to finish a group of three shrubs.

Hellebores thrive in shady parts of the garden.

Hellebores

Is there any plant more lovely than a hellebore? There are times, on cold February days, when it is impossible to imagine so. Hellebores grow willingly in sun and shade and are tolerant of any number of variations in the soil. Their foliage is upright and robust with flowers that offer a great variety of both colour and pattern within their petals.

Decades of plant breeding have given us some cultivars almost too beautiful to contemplate: the deep reddy-black lustre of the 'gun-metal' hybrids, the daintiness of the apple blossom group and the downright voluptuous showmanship of the 'Party Dress' hybrids take us through a wide variety of riches. Then there are the wild mountain hellebores, which grow at altitude through Southern Europe and into Asia. *Helleborus abruzzicus* has only recently been discovered in the mountains of the Abruzzo region of Italy and yet could win prizes at any garden show with its magnificent ferny leaves and large green flowers.

Choosing hellebores

Choosing hellebores is best done at a specialist nursery at flowering time, such is the range. A few pointers to consider: some of the taller hellebores such as *Helleborus argutifolius* and *Helleborus* x *ericsmithii* should be planted with plenty of space, given their tendency to form large, robust clumps. The most widely known and bred group are generally referred to as *Helleborus* x *hybridus*. This group is enormously diverse, covering all the colours mentioned above and it is vital to put your trust into the reputable, specialist nurseries who will sell you a plant of known character, raised at the nursery.

Bergenias

There was a time when *Bergenia* (elephant's ear) was the humblest of all garden plants and the source of much snobbery and derision from garden 'connoisseurs'. Then something almost miraculous happened. By working with the plant's tendency to colour red in the winter, plant breeders introduced a new world of wondrous foliage plants.

Cultivars such as 'Morgenröte', 'Bressingham Ruby', 'Eroica' and 'Eric Smith' have transformed our perception of *Bergenia* and when planted in large numbers (12 or more) they make a tremendous display in areas of dappled shade. Equally pleasing is that the new cultivars have dainty manners: gone are the bulky, coarse habits of traditional *Bergenia*, to be replaced by neat growth and tight, upward pointing leaves.

new perennial gardens

The meadow has come a long way. Britain's past is inextricably linked with cornfield meadows, where 'weeds' such as cornflower and corn cockle would bring extra work to the harvest and brought about the invention of seed sorting machines. As we developed weed-killers that only killed wildflowers, our cornfields became a more uniform, but less romantic sight.

Meadows have a deep hold on our psyche and it was inevitable that they would make a comeback at some point. Flowers growing *en masse*, with the subtlety and diversity that nature musters so easily, stir deep emotion and reaction, possibly more than a traditional border and there are many ways we can introduce this type of planting into our gardens.

In recent times, an exciting movement has developed out of the need for a less-ordered, more naturalistic planting that has brought together some truly exciting new plants and ideas. Some call it new perennial gardening, others prairie planting; it is a broad church with some clear common goals.

New approaches to plants and design

We are grateful to an innovative group of modern gardeners who have combined ecological rhythms and plants in new styles that are pure gardening in their display and artistry. Piet Oudulf, Noel Kingsbury, Nigel Dunnett, James Hitchmough and Tom Stewart-Smith are some of the planting and landscape designers who have pioneered this new approach. Working with perennials and annual meadows, they have turned some of the conventions of border design upside down.

Height ordering

Traditional borders work to a strict hierarchy: lowest growing plants at the front, tallest at the back. This effect creates a pleasant effect with the border rising gradually to a height of 2.5–3m (8–10ft) and all plants clearly visible. New approaches have challenged preconceptions on height ordering and shown how heights can be mixed. Grasses can be seen through and therefore can be planted in the front or middle of the border, for example.

Seasonal interest

Why should a border be just for the summer? New perennial gardening seeks to develop interest throughout the seasons. James Hitchmough's perennial prairies are massively diverse, comprising 40 or more species per 1,000m^2 (1093 yards^2). Rather than bare soil in the spring, a rich variety of different foliage and plant rosettes cover the ground.

Piet Oudolf's borders are famous for being as beautiful in the autumn and winter as they are in the summer. Rather than cutting them down after flowering, foliage and seed heads are left to acquire dew, frost and spiders webs, bringing an elegant, slightly melancholy element to the out-of-season garden. This approach is wonderfully beneficial for our precious soil flora. By maintaining cover for the soil over the winter, bacteria and fungi are sheltered from frost and rain. The soil can also hold far more carbon, too.

New approaches to annual meadows

Are meadows the best example of thoughtful gardening? When grown well, they need no water or fertiliser and are remarkably good at excluding weeds. They can be readily adapted to different soils and span many months of the growing season.

Nigel Dunnett's Pictorial Meadows were first created ten years ago and are now widely available from seed catalogues. They challenge some of the conventions of traditional meadows: they feature no grasses; they thrive on rich soil; and they combine native and non-native flowers. The effect is stunning; the high diversity and combinations of subtle natives against more vibrant 'exotics' create a vivid tapestry of colour. The recommended sowing density makes it difficult for weeds to enter the meadow and the flowering season extends over several months.

Some new perennial plants to try

The key to all these plants is a tough, self-sufficient attitude to life; they should not need staking, you will not be troubled by hardiness and they certainly will not need much summer water.

Echinacea: the North American cone flowers are standard bearers for the new perennial movement. Their upright habit, range of subtle colours and sheer toughness characterise everything needed for naturalistic planting. *Echinacea pallida* has pale white-pink flowers while the familiar *E. purpurea* (source of the herbal remedy) has petals of a much darker, richer pinky-purple. Recent breeding has thrown up some vivid new colours with cultivars such as 'Sunrise', 'Sunset' and 'Sundown' bringing dark, burnt yellows, oranges and reds.

Miscanthus sinensis **'Morning Light'**: there can be few more dignified, elegiac sights than this beautiful grass standing tall on an icy, misty December morning, the life long gone from its stems. Forming incredibly tight, discrete clumps, 'Morning Light' has the subtlest variegation that quietly illuminates the edge of each leaf blade. It is happy either standing alone or forming a narrow punctuation in a mixed perennial border.

Sanguisorba officinalis **'Arnhem':** also known as great burnet, its native origins give it a tremendous head start and it thrives on all but the poorest soils. Its wiry stems are a terrific asset, allowing it to punctuate broader or lower foliage, while being see through itself. Its flowers, claret red, raspberry-like clusters, glow over the skeletal structure of this plant in the first part of the summer.

Penstemon digitalis **'Huskers Red':** well-known garden plants such as 'Sour Grapes' and 'Raven' do not tell the whole story of the *Penstemon*. This is a huge genus with over 250 species, represented in both the New and Old World. In North America, *Penstemons* are found growing from damp prairies into deserts and their adaptability has seen them embraced by the naturalistic perennial movement. 'Huskers Red' is an unusual plant. A variety of *Penstemon digitalis*, it has dark bronze foliage, the rosette looking most striking against green at the beginning of the season. More traditional *Penstemon* qualities reveal themselves later in the summer: strong, upright habit, tubular cream-coloured flowers and a long, late-flowering season.

Anthriscus sylvestris **'Ravenswing':** another plant with a native head start, this is a dark, roguish cousin of the humble cow parsley. It has all the height and wiry, upright habit of its close relative, but it is the simple change in foliage colour, from green to the 'Ravenswing' deep copper that brings about a dramatic transformation. It is quite strong enough as a foliage plant, but when the same creamy white flowers are borne, the contrast is very bold and most garden-worthy.

*Allium schubertii's
spectacular blooms can add
drama to any planting.*

Rudbeckia fulgida var. deamii: another North
    American prairie dweller, this brings a rich, buttery
    yellow flower into play. Strong and upright, unreliant
    on staking, this versatile perennial works well in
    traditional herbaceous borders and naturalistic,
    looser designs.

Allium schubertii: there are many large-headed alliums
    around, but nothing quite matches the sheer drama or
    complexity of *Allium schubertii*'s vast globe flower or
    subsequent seed-head. Yet despite the extraordinary
    nature of this plant, it seems to associate well in
    naturalistic plantings, perhaps because its strong,
    squat stem holds the flower perfectly upright.

growing healthy plants

What part does propagation play in a book such as this? The thoughtful gardener propagates to maintain healthy plants, bring in new plants suited to their garden conditions and to minimise the consumption of resources in their garden.

Put simply, there are two types of propagation: vegetative and non-vegetative. The former creates genetically identical offspring while the latter will produce offspring different to their parents. Vegetative propagation includes techniques such as taking cuttings, while non-vegetative propagation is better known as growing from seed. Whatever we propagate, it is vital to choose a compost that will help our plants establish quickly and grow healthily.

what should I grow my plants in?

As mentioned on page 120, controversy lurks in the seemingly innocuous world of compost. Should we be using peat or not? For me, the choice for the domestic gardener is clear; unless you are growing specimens such as carnivorous or the fussiest ericaceous plants that cannot be grown without peat, there's no need to use peat for growing. The best garden centres and mail-order firms sell excellent peat alternatives that will not compromise how you grow. Here are the options available to you:

Green-waste compost

Green-waste compost is essentially the same stuff you make in your compost heaps or buy back from the local authority. Green-waste compost sold for propagation will have been sieved and graded to make a uniform product with consistent particle sizes.

Green-waste propagation compost is best used for growing on tougher plants, particularly herbaceous perennials and non-ericaceous shrubs. Its tendency to be slightly alkaline and salty precludes it from seed-sowing applications. Green-waste compost can also behave a little strangely with fertiliser and not all the nutrition you add may be available to the plant.

Derived-peat compost

A source of some contention, derived-peat compost is sold as 'peat with a conscience' under brand names such as Moorland Gold, and is collected from drains and sluices in upland areas. The water that runs off these areas contains small peat particles and has the same properties as harvested peat, while being a 'waste' product.

Derived-peat compost is peat and, just as a vegetarian would not eat meat of any kind, peat-free growers will not use it. However, if you are a carnivorous plant fanatic or have tried and failed to raise beloved ericaceous plants in peat-free compost, this is the best alternative.

Sylvafibre compost

A fancy name for pulverised tree, Sylvafibre is fast becoming the most readily accepted and best-performing peat alternative. When trees are processed for bark chips, there are many different fractions and products that result. Any products linked to the waterproof bark of the tree will hold no water, making them a good mulch but not suitable for raising young plants in. However, the internal sap-bearing element of the tree trunk can, if shredded into the right particle size, hold water in the same way as peat compost and is sold as compost for growing. Other factors stack up well in favour of Sylvafibre: pH is just below neutral, salt levels are low and the product is very stable. If your garden centre is not stocking it, ask why.

Coir compost

What is more destructive for the environment: harvesting a precious wildlife habitat like peat bogs or shipping coconut husks halfway around the world to grow our plants in? This is the debate that coir compost producers face and it is one that will rage on.

The benefits of coir are clear cut. It is a stable medium with a desirable pH in which to grow plants. It contains no natural fertiliser at all, so you can account for any nutrition that goes in and the product is extremely uniform and easy to handle, if a little spongey.

Counting against coir is its strange behaviour in relation to water. The surface of the compost can appear bone dry, even if it is heavily waterlogged and this makes judging when to water potentially very tricky. It also has virtually no nutrient holding capacity, meaning that fertiliser is required on a regular basis to maintain growth.

So, what should I be growing my plants in?

A mixture of all of the above. No, this is not a case of sitting on the fence: all of these composts offer different qualities and we should apply thoughtful processes to work out what is best for us.

Seeds and cuttings: this is where the inert, neutral qualities of derived peat and coir come into their own. Little seedlings do not want large volumes of fertiliser and would like to grow up in the sort of stable environment that these mediums can provide.

Potted on plants: something with a little more body is called for. If the plant is a tough, hardy tree or herbaceous perennial, green-waste compost should be fine, as long as you monitor nutrition levels carefully. Otherwise, the various grades of Sylvafibre will be excellent for any stage of a plant with roots.

Specialist plants: many ericaceous plants will grow in high-quality coir, green-waste or Sylvafibre compost blends and there are only a few (such as magnolia) that seem to struggle. If carnivorous plants are your thing, then derived peat is the best alternative to the harvested version.

cuttings and divisions

Cuttings

Cuttings are an ever-so-slightly magical part of gardening. What could be more wondrous than cutting off a small piece of a plant as big as a tree, popping it in some compost and watching a whole new plant develop? There is, of course, no magic, just a simple scientific process, but that never stops it feeling special.

Taking cuttings belongs to a group of techniques known as vegetative propagation, along with division and more advanced techniques such as budding, grafting and micro-propagation. A cutting is genetically identical to its parent plant and this allows a desirable trait to be multiplied again and again.

The most famous example of vegetatively propagated plants is surely the banana. Across the globe, essentially just one banana is being grown with any new plants just being copied from the parent. While this creates a wonderfully uniform product that tastes the same wherever you go and is easy to pack, what happens if a new banana disease appears? Which plants will be different enough to develop some resistance?

Contrast this technique with that of raising a new plant from seed. Here, the plant's DNA is allowed to express itself and genetic variety creeps in, so that a plant raised from seed has every chance of being distinctly different to its parent.

The thoughtful gardener will take cuttings to provide an insurance policy against winter cold killing tender, experimental plants, to regenerate old trees and shrubs that are no longer growing successfully and to multiply desirable plants for free.

Taking cuttings

Energetic growth will provide the best cuttings. Have a good look at the plant you want to propagate when it is flowering. Are there any stems that do not have flowers on, but that have grown strongly this season? A lack of flower indicates some spare resources within that stem and the unused energy could be very useful for a cutting trying to develop roots.

Cuttings fall into three main categories: softwood, semi-ripe and hardwood, although evergreen cuttings are normally treated slightly differently.

glasshouses can be
used to nurture
cuttings and seedlings.

Softwood cuttings: taken when the new growth of a woody plant can be easily bent with the tip of a finger, in the first half of the growing season. These cuttings are often taken from plants that need the most energy to form roots, but as the name suggests, they require very delicate handling.

Semi-ripe cuttings: taken from growth that is starting to harden, from late July onwards. When trying to bend the stems, some resistance is felt. The group of plants suited to this technique tend to be easier to root and include lavender, *Santolina* and *Helichrysum*.

Evergreen cuttings: generally taken in late summer or autumn from strong, non-flowering growth. They can be slow to root and are left to over-winter, grow in spring and need to be potted during the summer.

Hardwood cuttings: the only way to propagate some woody plants. They are best taken in the winter and grown in a covered frame, often with the end of the cutting in sand.

Taking and establishing cuttings

1 Search over the plant you want to propagate. Look for fresh, strong-looking stems that have not borne any flowers that season.

2 Use sharp and clean secateurs (or a specialist knife). If you have done lots of pruning with them previously, clean thoroughly using a natural disinfectant such as Citrox. Cut the full length of the stem; you can always make two or three cuttings from it.

3 The best cuttings are short and strong. Count two to three buds along the length of the stem. Make one cut below a bud and one above. The angle and quality of the cut is crucial to ensure the

future health of the plant. The bottom cut should be straight and just a few millimetres below the bud. The top cut should be angled and, again, only a short 'stub' created.

4 Rooting hormone can be useful for hard-to-root plants. If you know the cutting will grow readily, there is no need to treat; if you have had failures, then dipping the bottom cut into rooting powder or liquid could make a difference.

5 Cuttings should be inserted into a compost that drains freely. An ideal mix would be 50 per cent coir (or Sylvafibre) and 50 per cent silver sand or fine grit. Although stating the obvious, a newly taken cutting has no roots and will not use water in the soil. A moisture-retentive compost will only rot the base of the cutting. Make holes into the compost and place the cuttings around the edge of a pot or pan (a wide, shallow pot) where the drainage is best.

The lower cut should be straight and the top cut angled.

6 Your mission now is to stop the cutting drying out without rotting it. A propagator or even a plastic bag will maintain a humid atmosphere, giving it long enough to develop roots. The occasional squirt from a hand-held spray mister will help.

7 Things change as soon as a cutting develops roots. The best indication is growth, normally in the form of leaf buds expanding and opening. If you are careful, tipping out the pot will show whether some fine roots have started to form.

8 When the cuttings become strong plants, pot each one individually into a heavier, multi-purpose compost.

Divisions

One of the easiest ways to make new plants, dividing herbaceous perennials has many benefits. Any number of border plants can be lifted and then divided using some fairly crude horticulture, and this can allow you to increase numbers of a desired plant by 100 per cent.

Many herbaceous plants grow tired after five years growing in the same soil. They start to die out in the centre, leaving only fresh, strong growth on the outside of the clump. You can reinvigorate simply by lifting and dividing, dispensing with old, tired material and only replanting divisions brimming with energy and vitality.

Lifting and dividing gives a further benefit, which is unparalleled access to the soil that plant is growing in. Years of cultivation may have left it tired and compacted. Perhaps the drainage has become poor, or lots of dead plant litter has enriched the soil too much. With the plant out of the ground, a great opportunity arises to dig, add organic matter or gravel and generally improve conditions.

Select the right time of year. Most perennials are happy to be lifted in a period between the end of the summer and early winter (before it gets too frosty). Gardening wisdom suggests that more tender perennials, such as certain *Agapanthus*, *Salvia* and *Penstemon*, should not be prised out of the ground and split

dividing perennials is an easy way to make new plants.

open just before the onset of winter, with spring being a better bet. This all depends on how mild your garden is and the soil you are on. If it drains freely then there is little danger of the perennial's roots sitting in freezing water over the winter.

1. Gently loosen the plant by working around the outside of the clump with a large fork. Dig the clump out of the ground.

2. Is there an opportunity to improve the soil at this point? If your plant originates from a Mediterranean climate, then simply digging over compacted ground will improve drainage and some gravel could be added. For rich soil or woodland plants this could be the chance to add some organic matter.

3. Divide the clump using two similar-sized forks. Push the first fork deep into the clump with the curved back facing into the centre. Add a second fork, facing away from the first as close as possible.

4. Gently work the handles of the two forks towards and away from each other until you feel the clump parting. You may need to reinstate the forks occasionally if the clump is big.

5. Repeat the process until you have split the plant down to individual 'crowns'. This will comprise a strong stem bud and a decent-sized root system.

6. It may be tempting to return everything, but you should pick out six to twelve of the strongest crowns to replant the clump. It will look bare for the first growing season, but after this you will be rewarded with greatly improved flowering and much stronger growth.

growing healthy plants from seed

Growing plants from seed remains a joyful experience, even for experienced gardeners.

Is it the determination of the tiny seedling pushing up through the compost? The pleasure of planting something we remember as nothing more than a little seed? Or feeling in tune with nature when we collect the seed from the mature plant, in the knowledge that we will raise its offspring the following year?

There are more prosaic benefits to growing plants from seed. Economically, there cannot be many better returns than converting a packet of tomato seed into a full summer's crop. When it comes to buying plants, we may be restricted to our local nursery or garden centre. However, if we buy in seed, the world is literally our oyster, with an enormous range of popular favourites and botanical rarities available.

Getting the right plants for your garden

Growing from seed is one of the best ways to find the right plants for your garden. If you have identified the habitats in your garden and already know the types of plants that succeed in your conditions, then this is your chance to make special new additions that are as rare as they are successful.

Healthy seedlings.

Genetic variation

As explained earlier, there is every chance that seed will be genetically different to the plant it has been collected from. This may not be a problem; in fact many exciting new plants have emerged simply as a result of 'seedling variation'. If, however, you want exactly what is says on the packet, you will need to exercise caution.

The best seed companies (listed at the end of this book, see page 188) deal in two things: quality and honesty. Much of the seed they buy will have been produced using controlled pollination, that is, the parent plant has only been allowed to breed with its own kind and will produce the 'right' thing. If the seed company is happy their seed will come true, they will say as much in their catalogues and on the packet.

The honesty will come in when there is less certainty about the end result. Terms such as 'open pollination' suggest that the flower has had any number of suitors, leading to unpredictable offspring. If they are not sure what will emerge, reliable seed companies will tell you.

Ordering seed

For me, one of the great pleasures in life is ordering seed. Most catalogues arrive in the autumn and winter, and while dead leaves and snow may be swirling around outside, you can be transported to far-away lands, moving from the mountains of Chile to the grasslands of South Africa with the flick of a page.

If you have asked the best companies for seed catalogues, the first thing you will notice is that they understand what any thoughtful gardener wants: specific information about cultivating the plant. Each entry will tell you whether the plant likes to be dry or wet, in sun or in shade and whether it is hardy, half-hardy or tender. You may even find out whether it can take -3°C or -10°C.

Growing seed

All this diversity is a wonderful thing, but it will present some challenges when you sow your seed. High-end commercial seed is sold wrapped in a clay pellet (often impregnated with fungicide) and dyed, to make the seed consistent, disease-free and visible. This approach ensures that mass bedding schemes and commercial food crops have a 90–99 per cent success rate, as 'crop failure' cannot be tolerated. Much of this seed is available to us and we are most likely to come across it when ordering bedding plants or F1 hybrid vegetables.

At the other end of the spectrum is 'botanical' seed. From field and wild collected plants, this seed is as diverse as commercial seed is uniform and it gives a special insight into nature's numerous adaptation strategies and variations.

It is important to be realistic about germination for botanical seed. Some will come up like mustard and cress; others will leave you hanging on for a year or more before rewarding your patience with a couple of seedlings. The more you can glean about the special conditions the seed requires, the more chance of success you will have.

Some questions you should ask before you sow seed
What time of year should I sow it? Does the seed germinate in warm, hot or cold conditions? Will it germinate this season or does it need to go through a winter before growing?

Again, good seed companies will guide you through. The catalogue may be full of anecdotal advice (remember, they may have grown the plant themselves for the first time last year) or the packet may come with very specific instructions, designed to give you the maximum success rate. Failing that, if you still have questions, give them a call.

The main threats to seedlings have been mentioned elsewhere in this book (see chapter 3). Damping-off can strike suddenly and although fungicides can either prevent or revert this disease, 'inoculating' with *Bacillus subtilis* and good cultural practice will help in maintaining good health. Whitefly and sciarid fly are the two pests most likely to cause damage (see pages 98 and 101 for advice on dealing with them).

Sowing seed

1 Fill a seed tray, module tray or pot with a seed-sowing compost.
Try to seek out a peat-free alternative, such as coir (see page 156).
Make sure the compost is firm without being compacted.

2 Water before you sow and allow excess water to drain through.
Pass a watering can from side to side over the tray or pot. This
stops the big drips that come out of a watering can initially from
unsettling the compost. I always recommend watering in *Bacillus
subtilis* culture to provide immunity to the young seedlings.

3 Sowing should be governed by the size of the seed. Very fine
seed is best mixed with silver sand to show where you have sown.
Coarse seed should be pressed lightly into the compost. When the
seed is sown, cover with some sieved compost or vermiculite (a
mineral product). As a general rule, the depth of covering should
match the size of the seed, and none should be visible when you
have finished.

*Mix fine seed with sand before scattering.
Coarse seed can be pressed lightly into the compost.*

4 The seed tray or pot should be kept at a temperature appropriate to the seed, with a high level of humidity.

5 As soon as the seed germinates, reduce humidity. If you have seedlings under plastic or in a propagator, lift this off during the day. Seedlings are extremely vulnerable to fungal attack and a humid environment is perfect for nasty damping-off diseases to breed.

6 When the seedlings have produced two to three sets of 'true' leaves (not the initial seed leaves), it is time to prick them out. Tip the seedlings out of their container, loosen them with a dibber or pencil and transplant to a small pot. Seedlings need to be treated with great care at this stage: never hold by the stem, only the leaves.

Different types of seeds

Some seed needs soaking before sowing to break down the tough outer seed coat and speed up germination. This will be explained on the packet. More extreme variations on this include rubbing the outside of the seed with sandpaper or cutting a nick in the seed coat with a Stanley knife.

Some seed needs a special smoke treatment before it will grow. Some plants from Western Australia and the Western Cape of South Africa only germinate after bush fires and this 'smoky magic' needs to be replicated in our domestic glasshouses. Smoke seed primer normally comes as impregnated paper discs that are soaked to release a solution to water on to seed. When the plants that require smoke-induced germination are exotic wonders such as *Protea* and *Banksia*, a little extra effort may seem worthwhile.

169

A healthy lawn

Lawns are often regarded as an ecological 'black hole' and there is no doubt that a lot of chemicals can be used in the search for a perfect vision of uniform grass. The simple fact is that the grass seen on golf courses and the finest gardens is never arrived at by accident; invariably it will be the result of a full-time specialist following a year-long programme of work. However, achieving a lawn that is attractive and an effective backdrop for the rest of the garden can be done in a thoughtful way that does not upset the balance of the garden.

creating a healthy lawn

The most luxurious position to start from is when planning a new lawn. This offers the chance to create a system that will be tough, hard wearing and capable of plenty of healthy growth without our help. Choices abound when planning a new lawn but the key thing is to create a good 'rootzone' and to choose the right grass.

Lawns can be beautiful and ecologically balanced.

A healthy rootzone is the basis of a good lawn.

The rootzone

The rootzone is where the lawn lives and breathes. Grass needs good drainage and some quality loam-based soil to put its roots into. As this nirvana rarely exists, the best option is to buy something in. If you assume that the soil you have in your garden is going to form the base layer of your soil, then makes sure it is level and not too compacted. As lawns are best established in late September (mild conditions, warm soil, some rain around and the opportunity for grass to establish before the winter), there should be plenty of days to work the soil when it is not too dry or wet.

For a perfect lawn, buy in a ready mixed 'top dressing' to sow your grass seed into. The exact composition can vary and good suppliers will talk through the options with you. The three main ingredients of a good-quality top dressing will be sand, loam and organic matter:

Sand: ensures the rootzone of the lawn drains. Too much and the grass will never get to drink; too little and water will sit around for too long, which can encourage moss to take over.

Loam: binds the top dressing and gives anchorage for grass roots. Loam also holds water and nutrients.

Organic matter: brings beneficial soil microbes, many of which associate readily with good lawn grasses, more water-holding ability and humic acids to benefit soil health.

Creating a lawn from scratch

All major lawn work should be done in early September when the
soil is still warm and there is enough moisture for seed to germinate.

1 Remove all existing grass. This can be done by killing the grass with
a glyphosate-based weed-killer and then rotavating the surface. This
could be a lot of work and may best be done by a contractor. The
other option is to strip the turf off using a spade.

2 What is left will form the sub-soil of your new lawn. Make
sure it is not too compact and then get it level using a large
'landscape' rake.

3 Bring in a new 'rootzone' for your lawn. As a general guide, allow
for 40 per cent loam, 40 per cent sand and 20 per cent organic
matter. Measure your lawn to get the exact amount you need, and
allow for a 3 5cm (1 2in) covering of top dressing over the lawn.
You will need to keep a little bit back for covering the grass seed.

4 The top dressing should be spread evenly over the lawn
and levelled. Sow a tough, high-quality grass seed with a high
percentage of dwarf perennial ryegrass at the rate recommended
on the bag, generally around 30g per square metre.

5 Sprinkle a little top dressing over the seed, just enough
to cover it.

improving an existing lawn

If you do not have the time or resources to create a new lawn, there are ways to improve an existing lawn to increase its drainage and boost the quality and health of the rootzone.

1 Remove thatch, poor grass and weeds with a scarifier. Do not be alarmed if your lawn looks rather rough afterwards.

2 Extract as much of the rootzone soil as possible by hiring a hollow-core aerator. This will pull out cylinders of soil (which take a while to clear away so allow some time for this).

3 With the cores, thatch and weeds removed, this is a terrific opportunity to introduce a better-quality medium for the grass to root into. Buy in lawn top dressing; loose if you have a large lawn, bagged for a smaller area. Specify a top dressing with organic matter and high-quality loam and brush into the holes generated by the hollow core aerator.

4 Regular use of an organic lawn conditioner with beneficial microbes will gradually increase the biological life in the lawn and encourage it to be 'self-managing'.

With the right foundations, your ecologically balanced lawn will be straightforward to maintain. The key elements: good drainage, a healthy, well-aerated rootzone and high levels of beneficial microbes will always be required, so all subsequent work should support this.

Drainage

With the right base for the rootzone, drainage will not be a problem for the first few years of the lawn. Lots of traffic (from either feet or machinery) eventually causes compaction and this stops consistent movement of water from the surface of the lawn to the roots of the grass and away. With compaction comes a decline in the overall health of the soil with beneficial microbes and available oxygen in decline.

Remedies for compaction cover any size of lawn, from a domestic strip of lawn to Wembley stadium, but the principle is the same; mechanical penetration of the surface to allow rain and oxygen to access the rootzone of the lawn.

Decompacting a lawn

decompacting a lawn by spiking

Spiking can mean anything from spiked aerator shoes or a push-along rolling lawn aerator, to an engine-powered unit attached to a tractor. Spikes or blades on a rotating drum leave a series of small holes in the lawn that act as channels for oxygen and water. It is best to spike the lawn in several different directions to ensure the surface is fully decompacted. For most domestic gardens the best option is to hire, as the right machine will be expensive to buy and maintain.

Do not settle for the first local hire firm you find, however. You should make enquiries with your nearest public garden or park about which firms they hire from.

feeding a lawn

As discussed earlier, the traditional approach of applying lashings of nitrogen to a lawn to achieve a lush green grass is outdated (see page 110). Do you want to mow your lawn twice a week? Not only does this take time, but it will also use a lot of fuel and emit unnecessary volumes of carbon dioxide.

Composting is potentially the biggest issue of all: it requires lots of effort to compost a large volume of grass properly. In the height of the summer there is every chance you will not have enough 'brown' material to accompany an excess of grass clippings, leading to the infamous hot grey mush syndrome.

Lush, rapidly growing grass brings another problem: disease. Without enough potassium, new growth is soft and prone to disease. If the lawn is thick, the perfect damp environment is created for fungal spores to breed. Diseases such as *Fusarium oxysporum* (fusarium wilt), which manifests itself as yellow, then dead brown patches of grass, thrives in humid conditions and by preventing lush growth, it can be avoided.

Grass is perfectly green without using a nitrogen-rich fertiliser. Of greater importance is strong rather than quick growth and a little balanced nutrition ensures this. Minor nutrients such as iron and magnesium maximise photosynthesis and disease resistance.

The best turf foods are also rich in microbes such as mycorrhizal fungi and humus, and have organic rather than chemical origins. If the grass is strong and healthy from the rootzone upwards, the thoughtful gardener will have little need to intervene.

The best lawn fertilisers

Organic fertiliser: the thoughtful gardener occasionally needs
a strong stomach and an open mind, and there are no two ways
about it, the best organic fertilisers are derived from manures
or the animals that produced them. By the time it is in a bag, the
fertiliser has been processed to the point where it is far removed
from its origins, although I would always recommend wearing
rubber gloves and a dust mask when handling any organic product.
When buying organic lawn fertiliser, look for chicken manure or
animal meal as a main ingredient. Added to this will be a little NPK,
some trace elements and possibly some beneficial mycorrhizae.

Seaweed: rich in iron and humic acids, seaweed makes an excellent
mid-summer lawn tonic to combat disease and maintain healthy,
strong growth. Seaweed feeds, such as Maxicrop, come in a liquid
form and are sprayed on to the grass. The lack of major nutrients
in seaweed feeds means they are not the answer to a deficient lawn,
so it is best used in conjunction with an organic fertiliser.

wildlife–friendly gardens

The term 'wildlife garden' is, in the context of this book, something of a red herring. Throughout, the thoughtful approach has been to search out natural rhythms and patterns to garden more effectively but to my mind this is something different to wildlife gardening. This term can be associated with a look that sacrifices everything to create wildlife habitats, a look that often verges on scruffy with nettles and *Buddleja* grown purely because of their wildlife value.

This is where the green gardening debate can get lost as I believe passionately that gardening should always be about appearances. We must draw pleasure from the artistry of dynamically composed plants and detect the skill of the gardener, even if that skill is in knowing when not to intervene.

Beautiful, designed gardens support a host of wildlife. Garden plants can provide a rich source of nectar for pollinating insects, 'designed' borders can offer as much potential to be a wildlife habitat as a patch of nettles, and wildflower meadows can be planned around colour and structure.

We must treat wildlife in the same way as we approach everything else: as an integral part of the garden, not a strange annexe that has to be treated differently. We should apply the same thorough approach that we would to soil or compost and we should understand and accept the characteristics and limitations of our site.

structural diversity

Also known as a garden full of different heights, sizes and shapes, structural diversity delivers the key rules of a species-rich ecosystem: variety means lots of habitats, which in turn results in lots of species.

The BUGS (Biodiversity in Urban Gardens) surveys between 2001 and 2007 looked at the number and variety of different native insects living in a large sample of 'typical' flower-rich British gardens and concluded this habitat could sustain a great diversity of wildlife. It also discovered curious rarities that could be sustained by garden plants. The juniper bug is a rare moth in 'wild' UK habitats, but has been able to adapt to ornamental garden junipers, giving it a domestic-garden stronghold.

Given the densely populated nature of the UK, this places great responsibility on the urban gardener to provide refuge and habitat for insects and other wildlife.

nectar-rich plants

When discussing nectar-rich plants, *Buddleja davidii* and *Sedum telephium* are invariably the first plants to be mentioned. There is nothing wrong with either of these plants; in fact, they are attractive, vigorous and versatile. But surely we can try something else? Beautiful dynamic gardening and wildlife do not need to be mutually exclusive.

Lots of garden plants are nectar rich, and many native insects will happily feed from species alien to them. Here are a few interesting, nectar-rich plants:

Hibiscus syriacus: the large-flowered, hardy hibiscus grows well in most situations and its deep, open flowers gives ready access to nectar. A huge variety of colours is available.

Albizia julibrissin: a small, delicate tree from South and East Asia, also known as the Persian silk tree. It has fuzzy pink flowers that mark the end of spring. Attractive to butterflies and bees.

Echinacea purpurea: another great asset of the cone flowers is their ability to attract butterflies with ample nectar stocks.

Acca sellowiana: this glamorous Brazilian shrub is hardy against sheltered walls and its vivid scarlet flowers are so rich in nectar they make a good, sugary snack for hungry gardeners.

Magnolia 'Galaxy': this plant flowers several weeks after some cultivars, avoiding late frosts. It is a ready source of nectar for early bees. It prefers a slightly acid soil.

boggy areas and ponds

How much would it take for a boggy part of the garden to become a pond? A small pond encourages some extremely desirable natural allies into our gardens. Toads and frogs have an unerring sense for water and will use ponds to breed in late spring. They love dining on molluscs and

Frogs are a great method of snail control.

will quickly become your
most reliable method of slug
and snail control.

Dragonflies and damselflies will also turn up regularly at ponds that can
hold their water into the summer time and these beautiful insects are
also voracious predators, offering a free mosquito and horsefly control
service to the gardener.

borders in winter

Another positive contribution to creating a more wildlife-friendly
garden is not cutting down borders until late winter or early spring.
There are so many positive reasons for doing this. The soil remains
protected from winter damage, the soil's ability to hold carbon is
greatly increased if the foliage layer above it is not scraped off, old
seed and flower heads are viewed as a valuable source of food by
winter flocks of finches, and thick sheathes of dry, dead foliage
provide the perfect shelter for desirable insects looking to overwinter.

As we change our views on gardening and start to reappraise what
is beautiful, the collection of old stems, seed-heads and leaves take
on a landscape value all of their own. Frost holds on to the stems
in distinctive patterns, and winter dew and rain softens the shapes —
offering a viable alternative to bare soil or neatly cut-back clumps.

If the winter is severe, old foliage left on the plant will offer frost
protection, both as a 'sacrificial layer' to catch the frost and deflect
its attentions away, and as insulation for the newly developing young
growth at the base of the plant.

meadow areas

Meadow areas are not necessarily the highly designed prairies described elsewhere in this book (see page 150). They may just be areas of grass you cut less. Longer areas of grass are havens for insects looking for the right habitat to lay eggs and shelter from predators. You do not have to worry that this will only work on a 'field scale'; mini-meadows of a few square metres are very effective habitats.

Meadow management

Most meadows are cut annually, towards the end of the summer when the flowers within have set seed. Using a mower on the highest setting will take away enough grass while not damaging the rosettes of wildflowers establishing in the meadow. An alternative approach is to cut the meadow at different lengths in a patchwork or mosaic effect. This creates a varied habitat to support a variety of plant species and invertebrates. Most important is to remove the grass completely.

Meadow soil should be low in nutrients to ensure a level playing field for delicate wildflowers and grasses alike. If grass is cut and left to moulder on the meadow, then nitrogen leaches out, enriching the soil and encouraging plant bullies such as dandelion to take hold.

Wildflower meadows look stunning, provide wonderful habitats and require minimal maintenance.

In summary...

Your garden is a single ecological entity and, by applying the thoughtful approach to every job you do in it, you will achieve profound effects that go deep below the surface of your soil.

Never feel that being green or sustainable should be a penance or punishment. By using science and gaining a deeper understanding of how your garden functions you can create displays of the highest standards.

By creating healthy plants and soil, we may find ourselves intervening a little bit less, and this may give us more time to appreciate our gardens, or discover the next exciting design or plant we want to try. Does this sound like the gardening you would like to do?

glossary of terms

Bacteria: microscopic organisms that form part of the soil flora. Many have beneficial relationships with plants although some are pathogenic.

Fungicide: a product approved for controlling fungal diseases, such as rust. It can be of either chemical or biological origin.

Hardiness: a plant's ability to tolerate cold. Hardiness is either expressed as the minimum night temperature a plant can tolerate or in the hardiness zone (a US concept) the plant grows best in.

Insecticide: a product approved for controlling pest insects, such as aphids. It can be of either chemical or biological origin.

Meadow: plants of wild origin growing in a naturalised way. Meadows are managed by cutting and collecting.

Microbe: a microscopic, biological organism.

Mycorrhizal fungus: a fungus that spreads through the soil using long, slender tendrils. Mycorrhizal fungi have ancient beneficial associations with many plants.

Pathogen: a biological organism with the capacity to cause disease. In gardening, pathogens are typically viruses, bacteria and fungi.

pH: a measure of acidity or alkalinity. On a scale of 1 to 14, 7 is neutral, 1 most acid and 14 most alkaline.

Prairie: a wild habitat found in countries such as North America. Prairie planting seeks to re-create the plant associations and natural rhythms found in these habitats.

Protozoa: members of the soil flora, protozoa regulate bacteria numbers and release nitrogen.

Rootzone: the area of soil around grass roots in a lawn. The rootzone needs to breathe, drain and hold a healthy soil flora to sustain a strong lawn.

Top dressing: a material used to build and improve lawns, consisting of sand, loam and organic matter.

gardens to visit

Bog gardening

Marwood Hill, North Devon
The product of 53 years' inspired gardening from the late Dr Smart VMH, this is luxuriant West Country gardening at its best. Wonderful massed displays of _Astilbe_, _Iris_ and _Primula_ grow alongside the water that makes a constant feature throughout the garden. The sloping hillside planted with massed numbers of birch and eucalyptus is one of the great sights in British gardening.

The Beth Chatto Gardens, near Colchester, Essex
Presented with a wide range of habitats, from a bog to a gravel bed, Beth Chatto chose not to try and change her conditions, but instead chose the right plants to grow there. Her damp and dry gardens are seminal designs that have been highly influential. A small nursery sells plants grown on-site.

Dry gardening

Chelsea Physic Garden, Royal Hospital Road, London
A great example of thriving on poor soil, Chelsea Physic Garden's grey river sand hosts over 5,000 species. Its great strength is the wonderful collection of Mediterranean climate annuals, perennials and shrubs with wild-collected plants from Crete, the Balearic Islands and Macaronesia.

**Savill Gardens
The Great Park, Windsor**
Amongst its many highlights is one of the first dry gardens in the UK. A great variety of perennials thrive in this highly ornamental garden, growing in little more than gravel.

Shade gardening

Sissinghurst (National Trust) near Cranbrook, Kent
Is the Nuttery the most perfect woodland garden? In spring this is the place to see exquisitely detailed planting of shade lovers such as _Trillium_.

The High Beeches Handcross, West Sussex
Woodland gardening at its purest and most thrilling. A steeply sided valley planted with magnificent magnolias and rhododendrons leads down to flowing water. Bulb meadows flower in the spring. No tarmac, just a perfect landscape and inspired planting.

New perennial plantings

RHS Gardens, Wisley, Woking, Surrey

Embraces new garden styles as part of its ongoing mission to show us all aspects of modern horticulture. Around the Millennium Glasshouse is a 'steppe prairie meadow' created by James Hitchmough, showing the low-altitude floras of mountainous USA and China growing together with great harmony. Elsewhere, the long Piet Oudolf borders show classic elements of his design and are managed according to his year-round approach.

Sussex Prairies, Henfield, West Sussex

(open by appointment only)
The work of garden designers Paul and Pauline McBride, this showcase for their planting and design skills reflects many years spent working with new perennial gardeners and progressive nurseries on the continent. A wonderful dynamic sweep of planting opens up in front of visitors as they approach from a narrow entrance. There is plenty of subtlety here too, with thoughtful choices, making sure each plant plays a complementary role.

Gardening with tender plants

Abbotsbury Subtropical Gardens, Dorset

A dramatic exploitation of a mild, seaside climate. Abbotsbury mixes dense woodland garden and champion tree species, with open lawns planted with exotic shrubs and perennials from the Southern Hemisphere, including spectacular examples of Chilean myrtle trees.

Logan Botanic Gardens Galloway, Scotland

Nowhere else in Britain is the Gulf Stream exploited quite so expertly or beautifully. At a latitude in line with Moscow and Vancouver, this Scottish paradise grows an extraordinary array of tender exotica with South African tree ferns (such as *Cyathea dregei*) and Chilean shrubs growing large and lush in the mild, wet climate.

further reading

Adams, C.R., Bamford, K.M. & Early, M.P., *Principles of Horticulture* (Butterworth and Heinemann, fifth edition, 2008)

Brown, George, & Kirkham, Tony, *The Pruning of Trees, Shrubs and Conifers* (Timber Press, second edition, 2004)

Chatto, Beth, *The Damp Garden* (Orion, 1982)

Chatto, Beth *Beth Chatto's Gravel Garden* (Frances Lincoln, 2000)

Hickey, Michael & King, Clive, *The Cambridge Illustrated Glossary of Botanical Terms* (Cambridge University Press, 2000)

Ingham, Dr Elaine, *Soil Biology Primer* (Soil and Water Conservation Society, 2000)

Lacey, Stephen, *Gardens of the National Trust* (National Trust Books, 2008)

Lloyd, Christopher, *The Well-Tempered Garden* (Phoenix, 2003)

Lloyd, Christopher, *Garden Flowers* (Cassell, 2000)

Kingsbury, Noel, *Natural Garden Style* (Merrell, 2009)

Hitchmough, James & Dunnett, Nigel (eds), *The Dynamic Landscape* (Taylor & Francis, 2003)

McMillan Browse, Philip, *Plant Propagation* (Mitchell Beazley, 1996)

McLaren, Chris, *Ponds* (National Trust Books, 2008)

The National Trust, *Gardening Secrets* (National Trust Books, 2008)

Oudulf, Piet & Kingsbury, Noel, *Designing with Plants* (Conran Octopus, 2009)

RHS, *The Plant Finder* (Dorling Kindersley, 2009)

Thomas, Graham Stewart, *Colour in the Winter Garden* (Phoenix House, 1957).

Thompson, Ken, *No Nettles Required: The Reassuring Truth about Wildlife Gardening* (Eden Project Books, 2007)

Winch, Tony & Seton, Henry, *How to 'Cook' Compost: Making and Using Compost* (National Trust Books, 2008)

Recommended seed suppliers

B and T World Seeds
www.b-and-t-world-seeds.com
Based in France but happy to ship to the UK; huge range of rare plants.

Chiltern Seeds
www.chilternseeds.co.uk
A great institution. Their vast catalogue is full of exciting new plants, anecdotes and wit. Excellent advice on growing.

Plant World
www.plant-world-seeds.com
Nursery based in Devon with an excellent catalogue, strong on Chile and South Africa.

Silver Hill Seed
www.silverhillseeds.co.za
South African seed firm that has sold to the UK for many years.

Special Plants
www.specialplants.net
High-quality nursery and seed catalogue focusing on rare but ornamental perennials. Also sells Pictorial Meadow seed.

Thompson and Morgan
www.thompson-morgan.com
Familiarity should not breed contempt. One of the biggest firms, but still plenty of interesting plants.

Recommended nurseries

Crûg Farm Plants
Griffith's Crossing, Caernarfon, Gwynedd, LL55 1TU
www.crug-farm.co.uk
Bleddyn and Sue Wynn-Jones's trips to Taiwan, Vietnam, South Korea, Columbia and China have transformed the range of perennials available to British gardeners. Also available via mail order and online.

Long Acre Nursery
(Plants For Shade), Charlton Musgrove, Somerset, BA9 8EX
www.plantsforshade.co.uk
A nursery full of exquisite, shade-loving perennials and shrubs, grown to the highest standard in peat-free compost. Also offers a good mail-order service.

Marchant's Hardy Plants
2 Marchants Cottages, Mill Lane, Laughton, East Sussex, BN8 6AJ
www.marchantshardyplants.co.uk
Graham Gough is the consummate plantsman who has transformed a windy site with heavy soil into a dynamic, modern garden.

Phedar Nursery
42, Bunkers Hill, Romiley, Stockport, SK6 3DS
www.phedar.com
Specialising in hellebores, nurseryman Will McLewin's plants are wild, collected in specific mountain locations, true to 'type' and grown in local soil.

Priory Plants
1 Covey Cottages, Hintlesham, Ipswich, Suffolk, IP8 3NY
www.prioryplants.co.uk
Wide range of South African plants.

Pure Plants
Blackboys Nursery, Blackboys, Uckfield, East Sussex, TN22 5LS
www.pureplants.com
See perennials elevated to an art form. This nursery is all about plants with few distractions. Browse a great selection of really special, unusual cultivars (including field-grown trees and shrubs) and be guided by excellent cultivation notes.

Trevena Cross Nursery
Breage, Helston, Cornwall, TR13 9PS
www.trevenacross.co.uk
Plenty of South African trees, shrubs and herbaceous plants, this Cornish nursery represents the outer frontier of borderline hardy plant growing.

Witch Hazel Nursery
Callaways Lane, Newington, Sittingbourne, Kent, ME9 7LU
www.witchhazelnursery.com
Chris Lane's nursery and the home of witch hazel growing in the UK. Technically this is a wholesale nursery but plants are available for sale on nursery open days.

general suppliers

Agralan
www.agralan.co.uk
A leading manufacturer and supplier
of green products (including biological
control), Agralan make Revive (*Bacillius
subtilis* culture) and Citrox, and sell
direct to domestic and professional
gardener alike.

Alitex
www.alitex.co.uk
Supplies bespoke greenhouses
and glasshouses.

Bug Brewer
www.bugbrewer.co.uk
Firm selling compost tea percolators.

Bulldog Tools
www.qualitygardentools.com
Quality tools, including Japanese saws.

Cleeve Nursery
www.cleevenursery.co.uk
A nursery that sells its compost tea
to the public. Check their website
to see when they are making the
next batch.

Garden Organic (formerly HDRA)
www.gardenorganic.org.uk
The home of organic horticulture and
the most consistent voice in the green
gardening movement over the last 50
years. Their online shop and catalogue
has a wide range of seeds, fertilisers,
composters, biological controls and
natural pest solutions.

Harrod Horticultural
www.harrodhorticultural.com
The destination for the serious domestic
gardener (and professionals too). Harrod
Horticultural sells high-quality garden
equipment, including plenty of the tools
and products mentioned in this book,
plus a compost tea percolator.

The Green Gardener
www.greengardener.co.uk
Online retailer specialising in
biological controls for the garden.

The Natural Gardener
www.thenaturalgardener.co.uk
Online retailer specialising in using
sustainable, biodegradable, organic
methods and products in the garden.

Gardening Naturally
www.gardening-naturally.com
Selling a wide range of organic
fertilisers, physical pest barriers,
biological controls, biodegradable
pots and much more.

Two Wests and Elliot
www.twowests.co.uk
The best place for domestic glasshouses
and 'protected growing' solutions. Selling
quality high-end products, the Two Wests
(Christopher and Josephine) and Elliot
(their dog!) have a catalogue and online
shop and will help anyone looking for
propagation equipment.

Index